THE HANGING STAR

A JACK SAGE WESTERN - BOOK 4

DONALD L. ROBERTSON

COPYRIGHT

The Hanging Star

Copyright © 2024 Donald L. Robertson
CM Publishing

Books@DonaldLRobertson.com

The Hanging Star

ISBN: 979-8-9912601-0-7

✾ Created with Vellum

1

September 24, 1872

Since just past noon, thick clouds had rolled over Jack Sage, bringing relief from the hot summer sun he and his three horses and mule had burned under since leaving Las Cruces, New Mexico Territory. Across the rocky hills, downbursts of rain shafts, gray and silver in the sunlight, peppered the broken landscape. Now, nearing Silver City, the clouds above him were growing darker and heavier. Lightning flashed in the distance.

"Come on, Pepper, let's get a move on." His voice was urgent. He could see the scattered buildings not far ahead, but the wind was picking up from the southwest, and the clouds overhead were moving faster. The sharp smell of wet desert sand, lightning, and creosote bush tingled in his nostrils. He glanced over his left shoulder to the southwest. The Big Burro Mountains were disappearing behind the approaching heavy rain.

The town wasn't much to look at. It was more scattered than most he had seen. The houses and tents were thrown up haphazardly across the hilly landscape. Urging Pepper toward the patch of buildings that must signify the town, he had already passed several shacks and tents. A few had women and children staring toward the approaching storm.

Ahead, he could see the big wooden sign with the name Silver City Livery burned into it. It was swinging violently in the strengthening wind. He bumped Pepper again, and the big horse broke into a gallop, pulling the leads Jack held tight. The three other animals at the end of those leads leaped forward, and all four were galloping toward the barn. Lightning crashed into an outlying building less than a hundred yards from Jack. The small building exploded into flames. He could feel the hair on his arms stand out, and he felt it almost crackle with the electricity in the air. Then it was as if the bottom of the black clouds opened, and water dumped from the sky. He and the horses were instantly drenched. The livery disappeared in the blinding maelstrom, but he knew they were close. Racing through mud and near darkness, Jack yanked back on the reins to slow Pepper as the outline of the barn burst into his vision. The big rolling door was open, and they raced into the welcoming space.

"You almost made it," a big man with a blacksmith's apron shouted while he threw his weight against the heavy door, rolling it closed behind Jack and his animals. The roar of the rain on the roof made it impossible to be heard without shouting. "Seen you coming a ways off. Man, you was floggin' them horses. Then when that monsoon hit, you flat disappeared. I ain't hardly seen nothing like this since I've been here, and I've seen some hard rain in these here mountains."

Jack leaped from Pepper to give the man a hand with the doors, but they slammed into their stops before he could reach them. The man dusted his big hands off and turned to face Jack. He was at least two inches taller than Jack, who stood almost four inches over six feet tall without his boots.

He yanked off his wide-brimmed San Francisco hat and beat it against first one leg and then the other. "Whew-we, you're not kidding. That is a hard rain. Your livery disappeared when that stuff hit." The din of the rain decreased to the point it was no longer necessary to shout to be heard. "There'll be some flooding around somewhere."

"Yep, we get a lot of that. A couple of miners died last month. They got caught in an arroyo during a flash flood. Weren't no rain anywhere around them, it was up the mountains, but it sure washed them away." The man stepped forward and took two of the leads from Jack. "Here, let me help you. We can get these fine-lookin' animals in a stall and wiped down. Looks like they got themselves soaked, too, heh-heh. Don't have too much to say about it, do they? Just have to go where you want 'em to."

Jack nodded at the big man. "Yep, they need a good rubdown. You're looking at the best horses and mule a man could own." He rubbed Pepper, the soaked chestnut he'd been riding, water raining to the floor as his hand wiped across the big horse's neck.

"Name's Wilford Darby, but all the folks around here call me Tiny." He grinned, leading Smokey and Thunder toward a line of stalls. "I guess it ain't hard to see how I got that handle. Been big since I was a little tyke." Having headed toward the stalls with the two horses, he glanced back over his left shoulder, blond hair cascading from under his bowler hat. "Reckon you ain't been refused yore oats too often either."

Jack nodded back at the man while he led Pepper and Stonewall, his mule, to stalls. Stonewall pulled toward Smokey. "You got a stall that'll hold two? Stonewall and Smokey are bunkmates."

Tiny laughed. "Them mules can get like that. Sure I do. Bring him over here." Tiny tied Thunder and led Smokey into the stall next to him. Jack turned Stonewall loose, and the mule trotted into the same stall with Smokey and Tiny, shoving his head into the feed bin and latching onto a mouthful of hay, content to be with his longtime friend.

"You in town for the trial?"

Jack, stripping the wet gear from Pepper's back, shook his head. "Haven't heard of it. What's going on?"

"Judge Coleman, Andrew Jackson Coleman, is in town to try a few cases, but the main one is Jasper Rush, son of Elijah Rush, the owner of the Three Sixes. He killed a deputy U.S. Marshal. Shot him dead in front of witnesses. Wouldn't of been a problem, but he ambushed him from an alley with a shotgun. Guess he wanted to be sure the marshal was dead."

Jack shook his head. "Hadn't heard. Did the marshal have a family?"

"Yessiree, he sure did. A wife and a passel of kids. I think maybe six or seven. It's a good thing Rush shot him like he did. If he would've tried him fair like, Marshal Weaver would've taken him with no problem. He was mighty slick with a six-gun."

"You say the trial's today?"

"Yep. Taking place right this minute."

Jack hung the tack up and unloaded the few remaining supplies from Stonewall's pack saddle and then removed the frame. He reached into a pack and retrieved several of his home-made cookies, giving one each to Stonewall, Smokey, and Pepper. The three animals crunched away happily. Thunder stared over the wall of his stall at Jack.

"Just wait your turn, boy." He stepped back to the pack and retrieved three more, walked into Thunder's stall, and gave the waiting gray his cookie. Thunder, his lips rolled back, took it from Jack's hand gently and began to eagerly chew.

Tiny had been watching the little production. "Seems they like those things. What are they?"

Jack broke off a piece of one and shoved it into his mouth while handing another to Tiny. "Try it," he said between his crunching.

Tiny followed his example. He chewed for a moment before a wide grin spread across his face. "I can taste apple, oatmeal, and molasses." He began thoroughly examining the remainder of the cookie still in his hand. "There's something else I can't quite put my finger on."

"Carrots. Mix it all up and bake it. I shape them round, about three inches across. The size suits me and the horses. I usually have one a day myself, sometimes two."

Tiny laughed. "I'll whip up a batch. May even start selling 'em. I think the cowhands would buy 'em for their horses and themselves."

Jack nodded and went back to work rubbing down the wet animals. The rain had slowed to a light drizzle, but he could hear water running in the street. Thunder still crashed over the mountains, and the sharp fresh smell after a rain hung heavy over the high-country town.

While he worked on Smokey, his mind kept slipping to the trial and the dead marshal. Finally, he turned to Tiny. "I think I'll wander down and see if I can find a seat in the trial. I'll be leaving the horses here for a few days. Could you give them a little extra corn or oats? This has been a rough trip from Las Cruces."

Tiny looked up from Thunder. "You run into Indians?"

Jack nodded. "I did, passing through the Organ Mountains. I thought we were goners there for a bit, but we finally made it out."

"Yeah, those Apaches are deadly through there. Go ahead. I'll take care of these fellers. I've got corn and oats. They'll git plenty. Just leave your stuff. It'll be safe here." He grinned again. "Most of it, anyways. Those cookies are calling me mighty strong."

Jack loosed both his .36-caliber Remington New Model Police revolvers, checked each, and dropped them back into their respective holsters. "Help yourself. I'll whip up another batch if I need to."

Tiny had watched him ready his sidearms. "You expectin' trouble?"

Jack shook his head. "No, but I hear this is a pretty wild and open town. I'd hate for my epitaph to be 'He couldn't get his revolver out of his holster.'"

The liveryman chuckled. "Yep. That wouldn't do." He nodded toward the front of the livery. "Careful with the street. We can get a flash flood right down the middle of town. Mud gets pretty bad, too."

Jack headed for the smaller, human-sized door, opened it, and stepped outside. Tiny hadn't exaggerated. There was a river running through the middle of town. At its deepest point, it had to be maybe three feet deep, and the way it was running, if a man was knocked down, he'd wash a long ways before getting his feet under him again.

There was no boardwalk. Just rocks pressed into a walkway in front of the stores, and then mud. He looked at his boots. These were the best boots he had ever owned, and he was about to soak them in mud and water. He paused only a moment, shrugged, and stepped into the mud. Careful to stay out of the water's flow, he worked his way up the street. A quick thought passed through his mind. *I should have asked Tiny where the trial is being held.* But he dismissed it immediately. Just a few buildings north of him, a large number of wagons and horses were tied up in front of one of the saloons. He nodded. *I'll lay money that's where the trial is being held.*

With each step his boots slid ankle-deep into the muck and were held with the persistence of quicksand, almost pulling the boot off before it was finally released. He made his way slowly toward the crowded saloon. Each step forward brought a loud sucking sound. Reaching the saloon's rock walk was a relief. Jack paused, pulled his knife, and scraped at least a pound of mud from each boot. He straightened, sheathed his knife, and stepped forward to the swinging doors, listening.

It sounded like a claim jumper was on trial, and it wasn't taking long. The jury heard the three witnesses and the accused party, after which the judge asked the jury if they needed to adjourn. The men looked at each other, shook their heads, and the jury foreman said, "No, Your Honor, we ain't needin' to talk about it."

"Good, what's the verdict?"

The man looked down the two rows of jury participants. Jack watched each one nod. The foreman turned back to the judge. "Guilty as sin, Andy."

At the judge's frown, the foreman cleared his throat and repeated the jury's verdict. "We the jury of Grant County find this here claim jumper guilty as sin, Judge Coleman, *sir*."

The judge rolled his eyes at the foreman and turned to the claim jumper. The man stood after being prodded by his attorney. Judge Coleman eyed him and shook his head. "Andrew Beavis, you have been found guilty of claim jumping by a jury of your peers. Therefore, you are sentenced to one year of hard labor at the territorial prison. I must say, it is quite disheartening to see a rascal like you carrying such an honored name as Andrew." His eyes held the bedraggled crook for a moment before snapping to one of the deputies. "Take him to jail to await transport."

The marshal's deputy stepped forward, grabbed the man by his arm, and whipped him around, propelling him toward the swinging door. Jack stepped aside, allowing the two to pass, and waited for the judge's next announcement. Judge Coleman pulled a piece of paper from the top of the stack, read it over, and looked at a man sitting in the first row. "Marshal Hardwick, please bring Jasper Rush to this courtroom." The judge slammed his gavel down on the table. "Court's adjourned for ten minutes. Bar's open!"

Men rushed to both ends of the bar to get a drink. The judge's table and chair backed against the middle portion of the bar, blocking access for court observers, but making it simple for the judge to turn in his chair and call, "Gimme a beer, Bramley." The bartender already had a mug filled, ready for the judge, and slid it across to his waiting hand. Jack watched the judge blow a large head of foam from the beer mug and turn it up, drinking it half down before placing it on the bar and taking a breath.

A man, nearly as tall as Jack, sitting at the end of the second row, had stood and was pushing his way through the crowd toward the door. Passing Jack, Hardwick's U.S. Marshal's badge gleamed on the left side of his vest. He nodded to Jack and proceeded through the door to the receding waters running through the center of the street. Jack watched him pause, then jump over the stream of water. Moments passed. Jack was becoming concerned about the delay when the jail door burst open, and the marshal propelled a big young fella into the street. The prisoner turned, his face red, eyes bulging, and yelled, "You'll be sorry. My pa will see *you* hanging!"

The marshal reached the shouting man, said something inaudible, grabbed his arm, and thrust him toward the saloon. The young man jerked his arm away from the marshal and marched through the flooded street. When he passed Jack, his angry blue eyes glared at him. "Out of my way," he muttered, stepping into the saloon.

The judge, his mug tilted high to drain the last drop to his extended tongue, cut an eye toward the door. When the prisoner entered, he slammed his beer down on the bar, spun around in his chair, banged his gavel, and said, "Court's in session."

There was a murmur of displeasure from those at the bar, each man quickly tilting their drink up to finish it off before moving back to their chairs.

The judge's eyebrows drew together, and for a second his lips pursed as he watched the men remaining at the bar hurriedly downing their drinks. He banged his gavel again. "Bar's closed, Bramley. Pick up them bottles and glasses—now."

The bartender hurried to each man, retrieving shot glasses and mugs. He had to wrestle several to get their glasses away, but in a few seconds he had retrieved them all and nodded to Judge Coleman.

The young man entered the courtroom and dropped into the chair next to his attorney. He insolently stretched his legs, crossing them at the ankles, slouched down in his chair, and crossed his arms. All this was done while he frowned at Judge Coleman.

Jack watched the judge eye the young man as he was brought in. When he dropped into his chair, crossed his arms, and stretched his long legs, Jack shook his head, thinking, *He's making extra trouble for himself. This judge will not take kindly to any disrespect of the court. It won't make much difference if he's guilty or not. With that kind of attitude, out here on the frontier, he'll be stretching a rope before the day's over.*

The judge watched the prisoner, picked up the paper he had originally pulled off the stack, and began, "Jasper Rush—" The boy remained seated. His attorney leaned toward him and said something.

He didn't move.

The man's attorney looked nervously at the judge, leaned near his client again, and spoke.

No results.

Judge Coleman's lips pursed, and his eyes narrowed.

The marshal reached across the aisle and gave Rush a hard punch in the ribs with his fist. Everyone in the court could hear him. "Show respect for the court when you're being spoken to. Stand up."

Rush turned a beet-red face to the marshal. "I don't have any respect for this court, and you can go to—"

The blast of a Smith and Wesson .44 reverberated through the saloon.

The marshal remained stoic, for he had seen this before, women screamed, some men dropped to the floor while others grabbed their revolvers.

The judge, holding the smoking Smith and Wesson revolver, the muzzle pointed toward the ceiling, began shouting before the echoes of the blast died from the room. "You'll have respect in this court! If you don't, I'll throw you in chains. Do you understand me?"

Rush had dropped to the floor next to his chair. He slowly rose to his full height and remained standing. Trying to retain his insolence, though his hands, drawn into fists, were shaking, he said, "Reckon I do."

From his position, Jack couldn't tell if Rush was shaking in fury or fear.

The muzzle still pointed at the ceiling, Judge Coleman eared the .44's hammer back. "Your Honor."

Rush, glaring at the judge, said, "Your Honor."

The judge nodded. "Good." He waved the revolver toward the chair. "Now, sit." He waited until Rush had seated himself. The young man started to slouch as he had before, and the judge again waved the revolver, keeping his eyes on Rush. Jack could see the boy considering it, but finally watched him push himself erect in his chair. The judge nodded with satisfaction. "Good, now you can stand again while I read this."

This time, Jasper Rush stood along with his attorney.

The judge resumed. "As I was saying, you are on trial for the cold-blooded murder of United States Deputy Marshal and family man Chet Weaver. How do you plead?"

The prisoner looked at his attorney. The attorney whispered in his ear, and Rush said, "Not guilty."

There was an immediate and angry buzz in the room. Judge Coleman lowered the hammer of the revolver, laid it on the table, and, after grabbing his gavel, raised it high. The conversations halted. His old, steely gray eyes stared over the room. Satisfied, he nodded. "Be seated." He turned to the prosecution. "You may begin."

2

Jack had moved away from the door, slipping along the wall to an empty and darker portion of the saloon. He was near a side door, a short distance away from the mass of people crowded together in the makeshift courtroom. The courtroom offered no place for a man his size to comfortably sit. In the remaining area of the saloon, the tables were stacked on top of each other, legs jutting to the ceiling, leaving a narrow aisle to the bar and courtroom from the side door.

He found a lone chair that had been missed and moved it away from a table. Though he was trying to be quiet, one of the chair's legs scraped softly along the table leg. Jack looked up to see the judge's eyes glued on him and a frown on the man's face. Jack nodded, raised his hand slightly in apology, and sat. The judge gave a slight nod and turned back to the witness on the stand. The man was describing how Jasper Rush had stepped out of the alley and fired a blast from the shotgun directly into Marshal Weaver's back. This was the second witness.

This kid doesn't stand a chance, Jack thought. *I'm surprised he wasn't gunned down himself, but I imagine that shotgun had something to do with it. I wonder how they caught him.*

The trial moved on through two more witnesses, all with a similar story of having either seen Rush shoot the marshal, or seen him running away with the smoking shotgun. Throughout all the testimony, Rush sat glaring at each witness. Finally, the marshal was called and sworn in.

The prosecutor said, "Would you state your full name for the court?"

The marshal nodded. "Quinton Hardwick."

"And what's your position here?"

"I'm a United States Marshal appointed by President Ulysses S. Grant."

"As a United States Marshal, can you state what you know of the killing of Deputy Marshal Chet Weaver and the apprehension of Jasper Rush."

"I'll speak only to the apprehension. I was not witness to the murder." The marshal cleared his throat. "I found Rush passed out and drunk north of town. He had crawled up behind some brush along Silva Creek. He still had the shotgun with him. One barrel had been fired, the other was loaded. He attempted to swing it on me, but by the time he was alert enough to realize anyone was around, I was close enough to yank it from his hands. He came at me, and I knocked him out using the butt of the weapon I had just retrieved."

"Has he said anything to you about the incident since his arrest?"

Marshal Hardwick cleared his throat again and, while testifying, stared directly at Rush. "He said he wished he had seen me coming. 'Cause if he had, he would've done the same thing to me he did to Marshal Weaver."

Jasper Rush jumped to his feet and charged the marshal. A deputy tackled him halfway to Hardwick and threw him to the floor. The marshal leaped out of his chair when Rush flew at him, followed him to the floor, wrapped his thick arm around the prisoner's neck, and locked his head in a viselike grip.

Rush bucked like a loco, green-broke mustang, shouting, "I'll kill you too, Hardwick. Turn me loose and I'll blow a hole in you big enough to drive a freight wagon through."

Jack watched the marshal tighten his hold on Rush, gradually squeezing his throat closed. The prisoner gave a couple of spasmodic jerks, stopped bucking, and collapsed in the man's arms.

The courtroom erupted. Shouts of "hang him" reverberated through the saloon.

Judge Coleman sprang to his feet and began banging his gavel and shouting, "Order. Order in this courtroom."

Jack shook his head and thought, *At least I'm not involved in this mess. If that marshal doesn't protect that young fella, there'll be a mob hanging him tonight. All they need is time to get drunk and darkness.* He shook his head. *The boy probably deserves hanging, but it should come from the court.*

After a minute or two of pandemonium, the judge regained control of his courtroom. Gripping the gavel around the mallet, he swept the end of the sweat-stained, foot-long handle across the audience. "Shut up. Shut up, I say. If there is one more outburst from you people, I will empty this courtroom and close not only this saloon, but every saloon in Silver City for a week."

He glared down at the man who was held tight, and stabbed the gavel toward him. "Put him in irons, gag him with his bandanna, and put him back in his chair." The judge took a deep breath and seated himself behind his desk. "You'll not be disrupting my courtroom again, Jasper Rush."

Before they could get the bandanna around the prisoner's mouth, he shouted back at the judge, "You're a dead man, Coleman. When my pa hears what you done to me, you're the one who'll be hangin' from a cottonwood tree, not me."

The courtroom began to buzz again, but one look from Judge Coleman quieted it down. He stared at the now chained and gagged prisoner. No longer angry, the judge shook his head. "Boy, you just don't know when to keep your mouth shut for your own good."

Leland Abernathy, Jasper Rush's attorney, had been standing well clear of his client, the marshal, and the deputies. After Rush had been seated, he stepped forward. "Judge Coleman, it is impossible for my client to get a fair trial here in Silver City. I request he be moved to Socorro to continue his trial."

Judge Coleman let out a long sigh. "Mr. Abernathy, your client will get a fair trial today and will probably be hanged in the morning. These honest men on my jury will decide his fate."

"Your Honor, if you look at this jury, there is not a cowhand or rancher on it. It is solely made up of miners. My client doesn't have a prayer of receiving anything but a hanging sentence in this court."

The judge spoke in a low, threatening tone. "Mr. Abernathy, you, sir, are trying my patience. There's no cow folks on this jury because there weren't any around when it was selected. It's just that simple. Now drop it. The trial remains here." Judge Coleman cleared his throat and glanced back at the bar. He hesitated, licked his lips, and sighed. "Resume the stand, Marshal Hardwick." He looked at the prosecutor. "You may continue your questioning, Mr. Womack."

Hardwick picked up the witness chair, which had been knocked over in the melee, placed it back in place, next to the judge's table, and seated himself.

Jack had seen enough. Rush's act was murder, cut and dried. This jury, along with the townsfolk, was ready to convict and hang him. There was nothing more to see. He stood and started easing toward the door. The judge picked up his gavel, again by the mallet, and pointed the handle toward Jack. "Marshal Hardwick, I think the jurors have gotten a clear picture. You can step down, and would you detain that big fella trying to slip out of my courtroom?" He nodded to Jack. "You can be detained by the marshal, sir, or you can return to your seat until this trial is over."

In dismay, Jack's forehead creased with wrinkles. "Your Honor, I apologize for any disturbance to the court I might have caused. I was just leaving."

Judge Coleman nodded toward the chair Jack had just vacated. "Either have a seat, or the marshal will detain you. Which will it be?"

Jack shrugged and thought, *It's not like I have anywhere to rush off to. I might as well wait, but what the blazes is up with this judge?* Still wearing his puzzled expression, Jack jerked his head back toward the chair. "If that's where you want me, Judge, that's where I'll go." He turned, walked back, and sat.

The judge gave a slow nod of acknowledgment. "Thank you." His head swiveled to the marshal. "Go ahead and step down, Quinton." He looked at Mr. Womack, the prosecutor. "You're finished with your case, right?"

Womack was upset with the judge's interruption. "I am not. I still have other witnesses."

Judge Coleman let out a long sigh. "Maynard, are you trying to bury this boy? You've already put up enough eyewitnesses to hang him ten times over. Then you add in Quinton's statement. Don't you think you're overdoing it a little?"

Leland Abernathy, the defense attorney, leaped to his feet. "Your Honor, please."

The judge locked his eyes on the defense attorney. "What is it, Mr. Abernathy?"

Abernathy waved a hand along the length of the jury members. "Your Honor, you can't say such a thing in front of the jury. My client—"

The judge's thick, graying eyebrows jerked together. He leaned forward in his chair and glared at Abernathy. He began to say something, stopped, took a deep breath, and began again. "Mr. Abernathy, Mr. Womack, are you gentlemen prepared, at this time, to deliver your closing statements?"

The two attorneys looked at each other and then back to the judge.

Abernathy spoke first. "Judge, I have character witnesses yet to testify for Mr. Rush."

"I'm tired of this, Mr. Abernathy. There is no number of character witnesses who will make a hill of beans in this case. Denied." He glared at Womack, eyebrows raised.

"Yes, Your Honor. I'm ready."

"Good. Get started."

Womack cleared his throat and faced the jury. "Gentlemen of the jury, I will make this short."

A shout from the back came from an unidentified spectator. "Good. We're all thirsty."

The judge banged his gavel and searched the room for the violator. Finding himself unable to identify the rogue, his eyebrows again descended, and he addressed the crowd. "You folks are getting almighty close to an across-the-town closure of all saloons. One more outburst from anyone and you'll stay thirsty for a week. Do I make myself clear?"

There was an assortment of frowns and nods shot back to the judge. He continued to stare at the audience, finally nodding to Womack. "Continue, and it'd best be short."

Womack ignored the judge and the audience, concentrating on the jury. "I can make this short because the preponderance of—"

One of the jurors' hands shot up. The judge nodded toward him. "Yes?"

"Judge, you mind tellin' us what that preponder thing is?"

"Certainly, it means, in the prosecutor's words, the evidence is heavily weighted against the defendant, Mr. Rush."

The man nodded vigorously. "Thanks, Judge."

"Don't mention it. Mr. Womack?"

"As I was saying, the evidence has shown, without a shadow of a doubt, that Jasper Rush, while in a slovenly, drunken state, did, using a shotgun, blow a hole in the back of United States Deputy Marshal Weaver. As a result, causing the death of and murdering our good friend Chet."

Abernathy jumped to his feet, but before he could open his mouth, Judge Coleman waved him back down. Shaking his head, he reseated himself next to his client, Jasper Rush.

Womack continued, "It is your responsibility, under the laws of the Territory of New Mexico, to find Jasper Rush guilty of murder and to sentence him to hang by the neck until he is dead." Womack finished, nodded to the judge, and sat.

Abernathy was already on his feet, approaching the jury. "I know each of you as honest and law-abiding family men. Several of you have boys of Jasper Rush's age. There may be some who are friends with him."

The same voice spoke up from the gallery. "He's a rustlin' thief, him and every single one of his family. They ain't got no friends in this territory."

The statement was longer this time, and the judge spotted the speaker. "Marshal, have someone arrest and take Mr. Silas Potter to jail. He is sentenced to one week's jail time for not keeping his mouth shut and for disturbing this trial."

The man started whining immediately. "Judge Coleman, you know me. I'm a good man. Sometimes I just can't keep my mouth shut. I'll shut up and not say another word."

"You have gone too far this time, Silas. You've disturbed my courtroom for the last time." Judge Coleman looked back to the marshal. "Get him out of here."

Hardwick nodded to one of the sheriff's deputies. The no-nonsense-looking deputy quickly reached Potter and grabbed him by the arm, yanking him from his chair and sending the chair crashing into several of the gallery. Some gave Potter a dirty look while others glared at the deputy. Potter squawked and complained, but he was unable to slow the stride of the deputy. The two of them disappeared through the swinging doors, were gone for only a moment, and returned, backing into the saloon.

They were followed by a hulking man, his wide-brimmed hat seeming small for the size of his head. Thick black hair, smattered with dirty gray, thrust from under the tight hat, while tufts of coarse blacker hair reached from inside his ears. A large revolver, held in his thick fist, was shoved under the deputy's chin. His wool plaid shirt's first three buttons were loose, exposing, between his red bandanna and the open shirt, even more of the dark hair covering his neck and chest.

Armed men poured into the saloon behind the big man. Jack, sitting in the small niche between the overturned tables and back wall, watched, unobserved by the intruders. The side door burst open, and three men ran into the saloon with guns drawn. Jack started to draw, but there were too many innocent citizens in the room. Many would get shot if indiscriminate shooting began. He waited, silent and still, while the three men rushed past, dodging around the tables and ignoring him.

The big man shoved the deputy to the side, and several of the men following disarmed him. Jasper had turned around at the sounds of the commotion. His face lit up, and he started jumping, as best he could, in the chair he was chained to.

"Don't reach for that gun, Judge," the big man said, marching down the aisle toward the livid jurist. "I'd hate to have to drill your cantankerous old frame, but I will. Oh, I surely will." He marched up to the marshal, his men fanning out in the courtroom. "Gimme yore gun, Hardwick, and the keys to them chains."

The marshal wasn't fast enough for the man. He hit him with the barrel of his heavy .44-caliber Colt, striking Hardwick along the temple with the massive barrel. The lawman collapsed to the floor, blood gushing from a deep gash along the side of his head.

This is getting out of hand, Jack thought. Somehow the gunmen had missed his massive bulk in the shadows. He drew both of his revolvers and, still seated, waited.

"Elijah," Judge Hardwick said, addressing the man who had just pistol-whipped the marshal, "you won't get away with this. You'll hang right alongside your worthless son."

Elijah Rush had bent over and yanked the marshal's gun and key ring from his belt. He straightened and turned his weapon toward Coleman. "Andy, you've gotten way too big for your britches since they made you a territorial judge." He tossed the keys to one of the cowhands. "Unlock my boy, and get that blasted bandanna out of his mouth."

The man deftly grabbed the key ring out of the air. "Sure thing, boss." The cowpuncher slid his hand between the bandanna and Jasper Rush's cheek and yanked.

The instant the bandanna came free, Jasper began yelling, "Git me loose from here. Git me loose. I need a gun."

While the cowhand worked at the locks, Jasper bounced in the chair, yelling, "You're a dead man, Coleman. I'm gonna drill you right where you sit. You'll never see the light of day again." When the chains fell free, he leaped to his feet and grabbed at the gun in the cowhand's holster.

"Leave it be, Jasper," Elijah Rush shouted at the boy. "You've done enough already."

"No, Pa, I'm gonna kill him and Hardwick. They deserve it." The boy was jumping from one foot to the other, giving the cowhand who had released him but retained his gun a look that could kill. "Gimme that gun!"

He lunged for the holstered revolver again.

Elijah Rush had moved closer, and he slapped his son with a massive open hand, the blow rocking the solid young man. "I said leave it be, boy, and I mean it. Now let's get out of here." He motioned his head toward the door. "You men who came in the side door, get to your horses and ride."

The three men backed out the side door and pulled it closed behind them.

Judge Coleman sprang to his feet behind his desk. "Elijah,

you don't want to do this. You're already in trouble. Don't take it any further. You've got a bad seed in this boy. He's no good. Let the law take care of him, but don't get dragged down with him."

The older Rush, who was shoving his son up the aisle following his men, turned back to the judge. "Coleman, you'd best shut your mouth. I'm right on the edge of turning this boy loose on you, so don't push me."

Jasper had stopped at the door. "Do it, Pa. Shoot the old crow bait. Shoot him!"

Rush hurried to the door and shoved his son outside. He was the last man to the door. "Anyone comes out this door within the next five minutes is dead." He spun and pushed through, his huge frame disappearing.

There was a universal sigh from the assemblage. Jack could feel his body relax. *We dodged that bullet,* he thought. Just as the thought cleared his mind, the swinging doors of the saloon burst open to the shout from Elijah Rush, "Don't do it, Jasper!"

Jack saw the young man leap through the swinging doors, a .44-caliber Navy Remington in his right hand. The weapon was up and hunting for Judge Coleman. Jack's body reacted like it had many times before. His guns were already out. The boy was thirty feet away, standing in the sunlight streaming through the saloon doorway. Jack's right arm came up and straightened, like he was fighting a duel. There were others in the room. He had to make sure of this shot. He settled the sights of his .36-caliber Remington New Model Police revolver on the killer's temple and squeezed the trigger. His shot sounded a fraction before the shot from Rush's Remington. The bullet crashed into Rush's head exactly where it had been aimed.

He fell back through the swinging saloon door. Jack heard an anguished cry from outside the building, "Nooo." It combined with a woman's scream inside the courtroom. He leaped for the door. There was a fusillade of gunfire from outside, puncturing the thin walls of the saloon. He kept moving. Passing the door, he fired both of his revolvers.

He was fast, almost like a machine. He had owned the little .36-caliber weapons for several years, and they were like extensions of his body. His finger would squeeze the trigger. In the recoil, as the barrel rose, his big thumb fell over the hammer to pull it back to full extension, and when the muzzle came back down in alignment again, it was cocked and ready to fire.

Jack was tall, at least three and a half inches above six feet without his boots on. He towered over the top of the swinging doors. He fired round after round at the mounted cowhands as they desperately tried to turn their horses to get far away from the flying lead. One slumped in the saddle, another grabbed him, while another tumbled to the ground. They raced down the street, mud and water flying from the heels of their mounts. Jack could see one man down in the street, and Jasper lying on the rocks in front of the saloon. He watched for only a moment, then turned back into the room. *How many people are hurt?* Jack thought, followed by, *That crazy kid. That has to be the answer. The kid was crazy.*

3

Three people had been shot, two women and one man. Fortunately, the doctor had been in the courtroom and unharmed by the flying bullets. The judge was directing the moving of those injured to the open area at the side of his desk. There, the injured spectators were laid out alongside Marshal Hardwick, who had not yet regained consciousness.

Dr. Pratt worked on one of the women while the spectators milled about in the room like a herd of cattle without the lead steer. People were crowding around the injured. The doctor looked up, his mouth turned down and brow furrowed. "Judge, get these people out of here. I need room to work, and someone go get my wife. Tell her to bring my kit."

The judge looked at a younger man, about the age of Jasper Rush. "Billy, go get Martha and tell her what the doc said."

The young man nodded and dashed from the saloon. More people were trying to crowd in from the street to see what had happened. The judge turned to the two deputies. "Get these folks out of here, and don't let anyone else in except the doc's wife."

The deputies went to work clearing the saloon. Judge Coleman banged his gavel twice on his desk. "Probably not worth mentioning, folks, but this trial is over." He turned to the men who had been on the jury. "Thanks for your service, men."

One of them spoke up. "Don't mention it, Judge." He looked at the bar and licked his lips. "Is the saloon open for business?"

Coleman nodded at the bartender. "It's open, but don't crowd the doc, here. Let him have all the room he needs."

"Thank you kindly, Andy," the same man said as he stepped up to the bar. "Gimme a beer."

Several of the men moved to the bar while others unstacked the tables, placing them in their previous locations about the room. They also moved the chairs back to the tables. At the same time, since the bar had opened, the ladies hurried from the premises, many accompanied by their husbands.

Only a short time passed before the young man was back with Mrs. Pratt. He was carrying a large leather case. She rushed to the doctor's side. "What can I do?"

The doctor's response was lost to Jack as the judge stepped up to him. "Mr. Sage, I am Judge Coleman. Could I interest you in a drink?"

Jack nodded to the wounded still on the floor. "What about those folks and Marshal Hardwick?"

"The doc will take care of them. I told him if he needs any help to give me a holler, and as soon as the marshal comes to, he'll let me know. Now how about that drink?"

"I'll join you, Judge, but I'm not much on drinking. Maybe a cup of coffee."

The judge nodded to Bramley, the bartender. "A beer and a coffee."

Bramley waved his acknowledgment, and Coleman guided Jack to a table. Jack removed his California hat, laid it on the table next to him, and combed his hair back with his hand. "So, Judge, you know me, but I can't say as I've ever met you. Also, I don't see anyone rushing around trying to get a posse together to get after that Rush fella."

"Only someone dead-bent on suicide would take after Elijah Rush and his bunch. They're snakebite mean. Rush knows this country like his own barnyard, and he'll set up an ambush for any who follow. No, it'll take more than a town posse to bring them in."

A man shoved through the saloon's swinging doors and called, "Doc, one of Rush's men is still alive out here, but he looks to be bad off."

Dr. Pratt rose from the man he was working on. "Move him to a dry spot. I'll be out there when I can."

"Sure thing, Doc." The man looked around until he spotted the judge. "Andy, what do you want us to do with Jasper's body?"

The judge turned in his chair. "He's dead, isn't he?"

"Oh, yeah. He's got a big hole through his head. He's about as dead as a feller can git."

"Well, go get Wickham. He'll take care of him. Tell him to bury him in boot hill, and the territory will pay for it." He turned his attention back to Jack. "Now where was I?" He picked up his beer, took a long drink, set the mug down, and wiped the foam from his mouth with his sleeve. "Oh, yeah, how I know you." He nodded as if agreeing with himself and looked at Jack. "El Paso. I saw you in El Paso a few months ago when you were with the rangers chasing those kidnapped girls. I was over conferring with Marshal Ruff, who had caught a couple of folks we were after. They were going to prison, so I wanted to identify them and let the marshal know we wanted them after Texas was finished with them. A little more time in prison won't hurt those fellas." He picked up his beer, emptied the mug, and waved it at Bramley.

The bartender nodded, filled another mug, and headed to their table. He set it down and motioned toward the doc, who was overseeing the removal of the injured folks from the saloon. "Marshal's starting to wake up, Judge, but the doc said he's kinda worried about him. He's all woozy and can't stand."

The judge took a drink of the fresh beer, slower this time,

wiped his mouth again, and set the mug down. "He'll be all right. Hardwick's hard head would protect him against just about anything. Tell the doc to send him to me when he's up and feeling better." He nodded his dismissal. "Thanks, Lester. Give us some privacy. I need to talk to Mr. Sage."

Bramley picked up the empty mug, said, "Sure, Judge Coleman," and turned back for the bar.

"As I was saying. I saw you in action in El Paso when you were with the rangers. Asked about you, and found out you've built yourself quite a reputation."

Jack shook his head. "A reputation is the last thing I'm looking for. I just help out occasionally when help is needed and I have time." The last he said with a bit of emphasis, for Jack already had plans for his time in this part of the country. His ranching money was beginning to run low, and, though he had invested with Bronco Fenn and Montana Huff in their Texas ranch, he had yet to receive any payments from them. He wasn't worried about his friends and their success, but in the meantime, he thought he'd try his luck prospecting, and Silver City seemed to be a likely place. If it didn't work, he'd figure something out. He always did.

Jack could see the judge pick up on his time emphasis.

The judge sat thinking and staring out the saloon's window. "Reckon you might *make* some time right now?"

"Judge Coleman, now doesn't work for me. I'm out here to do a little prospecting on my own. If I do some good, then I might be available, but now just won't work out."

The judge shook his head. "That's not good. We're in mighty bad shape, what with Marshal Hardwick gettin' banged upside the head. The Marshal Service in this territory was already short before Chet Weaver was killed. Now, with Hardwick injured, I'm suffering a real loss. I surely am." He took another sip of his beer.

Jack lifted his cup again. The hot brew was strong and gave off an enticing aroma. He allowed a little of it to flow past his lips and across his taste buds. The black, bitter concoction warmed and invigorated him as it flowed down his throat, burning slightly. He swallowed quickly, feeling the heat all the way to his stomach. *I'm not giving in to anything,* he thought. *I've got to try my hand at this prospecting. I've never depended on luck before, but maybe it'll smile on me. It's for sure and gone, if I don't try, I won't find anything.* He slid his chair back and stood. "Sorry, Judge Coleman, maybe another time. I'm through catching bad men for a while."

"Isn't there some possible way I might talk you into helping us out? I can appoint you a United States Deputy Marshal right now. I'll make you a special deputy so you don't get stuck with setting up courts or collecting taxes. It'll be only for the sole task of bringing in Elijah Rush and his bunch. The pay's not great, but you won't do bad. What do you say? Can you help me?"

Jack looked down at the judge's solemn face. The man was sincere, and he needed help, but Jack had been around long enough to know the system would continue to work with or without him. The judge would find someone else who'd be just as good or even better. He picked up his wide-brimmed San Francisco hat and set it on his head. "Judge, trust me when I tell you I'd like to help, but unfortunately it's not in the cards. I've got to give this prospecting a try. If it doesn't pay off after a few months, then you or Marshal Hardwick can look me up, but for now I've got an itch, and I've got to scratch it." He nodded to the jurist, turned, and walked through the batwing doors, stepping out into the cool, almost chill afternoon.

The clouds, building again over the mountains to the west and north, looked black in the slanting sun. Jack lifted his right hand to his front brim and his left to the back and leveled his hat until it felt just right. He looked around and walked slowly through the mud to the hotel. The thick mud sucked at his boots. The river that had been flowing down the middle of the street had disappeared, but the width of the thoroughfare, along with the alleys, was a quagmire. Making it to the Gold Strike Hotel, he grasped the rail along the side of the three front steps leading up to the porch and entryway. He pulled one foot out of the muck and scraped it on the edge of the first step. A big clump of mud splatted to the ground. Next, standing on the step, he pulled the other foot out of the mud and repeated his action.

Satisfied, Jack straightened, walked up the steps, and entered the hotel. Once inside, he stopped to look around. A long brocade divan sat on each side of the entryway, funneling the guests toward the check-in desk. Once past the divans, a patron could turn between the check-in desk and the end of the left divan and enter the dining area. Jack figured it was a good sign he could see several people sitting at tables. He could also hear conversation and dishes clinking. The sound reminded him he was hungry. The last meal he'd had was venison jerky for breakfast. The thought caused his stomach to growl. A well-dressed, but tough-looking gentleman, sitting on the couch and reading a newspaper, looked up, gave him a sardonic smile and a nod.

Jack returned the favor. "Have you eaten in the hotel?"

The man lowered his newspaper and raised dark brown eyes, almost coal black and just as hard, to Jack. "I have, and I would definitely recommend it. The food is good, and the waiters are pleasant and quick. Your glass will not empty."

Jack took a quick measure of the man, tough, confident, and hard—maybe mean, but that was to be determined. "Thanks." He began to step past, and the man stood, extending his right hand. "Name's Henry Marsden. My friends call me Hank. Would you care for company with dinner?"

Jack looked at the man for a moment, took the hand, and shook it. Marsden's handshake was strong, to go with his size, but not overpowering. He wasn't as tall as Jack, but he was at least as wide, maybe wider, with a grip like a vise, but it was obvious to Jack he wasn't interested in asserting his manhood with his handshake. Marsden gave a quick shake and released Jack's hand.

"Sure, I'm new here. I can use a little company. I'll warn you though. I'm sparse with words."

Marsden threw back his head and laughed. "Good, then you won't be interrupting me. I tend to speak often and lengthy. I'm afraid if you're used to the silence of the plains, I might be a little overpowering."

"Not a bother to me as long as you don't expect an answer. Name's Jack Sage."

Marsden turned his head slightly, examining Jack. "Jack Sage. You the lawman?"

"I've been a lawman."

The two men walked into the hotel dining room. A waiter carrying two menus stepped forward to greet them. "Good afternoon, Mr. Marsden. Would you care to sit at your regular table?" Without receiving an answer, the waiter turned toward the front of the restaurant. Jack looked it over. The only two tables there were located adjacent to the window, allowing a good view of the street and the tables' occupants.

"Pardon me."

The waiter paused, turned, and stared at Jack, his chin slightly elevated. "Yes? May I help you, sir?"

Jack turned to his new acquaintance. "Let's sit in the back. I have an aversion to sitting by windows."

Marsden nodded. "Fine with me."

The waiter, a little huffy, changed directions and guided the men to the back. Jack, quite comfortable sitting in the rear of the restaurant with his back protected by two walls, was pleased with the change in tables.

The waiter seated them and handed each man a menu. Jack took a quick scan and looked up. Surprised, the waiter asked, "You've made up your mind, sir?"

"I have. I'd like the meatloaf, mashed potatoes, and green beans. Are those beans fresh?"

The waiter smiled. "Yes, sir. They are grown right here in Silver City. I think you'll enjoy them. Anything to drink?"

"Coffee."

The waiter looked at Marsden. "Sir?"

"I will have a piece of your delicious peach pie and coffee, Louis."

"Louis," Jack said, "my name is Jack Sage, and you'll probably be seeing me in here quite often. This table is where *I'd* like to sit if it's unoccupied. Sitting by the window can be hard on a man's health." Jack handed Louis his menu. "Why don't you also give me a piece of that pie."

Louis inclined his head to Jack. "Yes, sir, I understand, and I'll have your meal out shortly, Mr. Sage."

"Thanks." Jack removed his hat, laid it carefully in the empty chair to his left, and stretched his long legs to one side of the table. "It feels good to stretch out."

"Yes, I'm sure it does after that ride from Las Cruces and the escape from Apaches."

Jack's eyebrows rose, and Hank Marsden gave a short laugh. "Think nothing of it. Within thirty minutes of you arriving in town, everyone knew you had ridden in from Las Cruces, got away from the Apaches, your name is Jack Sage, and you have a passel of horses with you, not to mention a mule."

Jack shook his head. "So what you're telling me is not to say anything in front of Tiny that I don't want broadcast across the countryside?"

Marsden returned the head shake. "Not really. Tiny can keep a secret very well. It's the general stuff that gets passed along. You tell him something in confidence, and it will never pass his lips. But you just ride in, and he'll spread the news." Marsden took a swig of his coffee. "They make good coffee here, too."

Louis brought out Jack's meal and Marsden's pie. To Jack, he said, "I'll bring your pie later." He stepped back from the table. "Anything else, gentlemen?"

Jack looked at Marsden, then shook his head to Louis. "Nope, I think we're set. Thanks."

He picked up his fork and dug in.

Marsden leaned forward. "Jack, you know you're in trouble, don't you?"

"How's that?"

Marsden's dark eyes stared at the big man. "You killed Elijah Rush's youngest son. Don't you understand? He'll be hunting you. Right now, he wants to put you in the ground. That's his goal. He's aiming to kill you."

Jack was working his way through the mashed potatoes, meatloaf, and green beans. Nothing was going to upset him, at least not until he finished eating. He finished a bite of mashed potatoes and, after swallowing, said, "Elijah Rush came into town today to create trouble. Obviously he's been lording it over this town for quite a while. It's time the merchants and citizens get together and get rid of the likes of him. That's what the law is all about. Marshal Hardwick will be back on his feet in no time. Listen to him, do what he says, and you won't have to worry about Rush or anyone else." He went back to eating. Finishing his meal, he leaned back in his chair.

Louis stepped up with Jack's peach pie, picked up his dishes, and moved quickly from the table.

Jack gazed at the pie. It smelled deliciously enticing. Bright, fresh, yellow peaches embedded in a thick filling oozed from between the crisp, flaky crust. It looked like the waiter had brought him almost a quarter of the pie. He sliced off the tip, and steam rose toward him. He grinned at Marsden. "Looks like your peach pie choice was bang on."

Marsden shook his head, still concerned about Rush. "Jack, you don't know this man. Today, you killed his youngest son. He won't stop until you're dead."

Jack held the pie on the end of his fork and blew on it to cool it just a bit. Then he slid the sweet peaches and crust into his mouth. Still hot, he moved it around quickly to keep from burning his cheeks or tongue. Savoring the taste, he allowed it to dissolve and at length swallowed the piece while cutting off another chunk.

Before lifting the fresh bite to his mouth, he replied, "Not if he has an understanding of the law. He saw Jasper come back into court with the sole purpose of killing the judge. What do you think he expected? You think he thought someone would pin a medal on his son's chest?" Jack answered his own question. "No, I'm sure he didn't. In fact, I think he knew there was a possibility his son could be killed. The reality is that it's his own fault, and he'll have to accept responsibility for it.

"However, I don't think he'll come after me. That changes things up entirely if he tries to kill me or sends someone. He's already looking at jail time for shooting up the courtroom and injuring citizens. If he pursues me, it'll be him going to boot hill or prison, not someone else."

Marsden shook his head. "You don't know him. He'll send out his riders. He has some good hands working for him, but he also has gunmen. Plus he has his other sons. He'll send them and those gunmen. They'll kill you."

Jack took another bite of the pie. His face lit with pleasure. "That is mighty good. I haven't tasted fresh peach pie in a long while. I need to let the chef know how tasty this is."

Marsden stared at Jack, incredulity written across his face. "Peach pie? I'm talking about your murder, and you're talking about peach pie?"

Jack looked across the table at his new friend. "You do talk a lot, don't you?"

4

The two men stepped back into the hotel lobby. Jack moved to the front desk with Marsden alongside and was greeted by the clerk. He was a tall, slim young man, wearing gray wool trousers, a white shirt, and a red and white striped bow tie. "Sir, may I help you?" The young man glanced at Jack's companion. "Good afternoon, Mr. Marsden."

"Afternoon, Blake. How's my daughter doing?"

Blake smiled at Marsden's inquiry. "Quite well, sir. You must come for supper. I know she'd love to see you."

"How about tonight? Would that work?"

Blake grinned. "Yes, sir, it would make her day. Thank you."

Jack waited patiently while the two carried on their conversation. Blake turned back to Jack. "Sorry for the delay, sir. Mr. Marsden is my wife's father."

"Not to worry. I need a room. Let's make it for a month. I'll be in and out and may be gone for a week at a time. I'll be leaving some things in the room."

"Certainly, sir." Blake was all business. "Anything you leave in your room will be safe." He slid a ledger to Jack and pushed a pen across to him. Jack filled in his name, projected date of departure, and spun it around to Blake. The clerk glanced at the ledger and noted the departure date, November first. "How would you like to pay, Mr. Sage, daily, weekly, or monthly?"

"How much is it?"

"If you pay daily, it's a buck twenty-five. Weekly is eight dollars, roughly a dollar fourteen a day, and monthly is thirty-one dollars, a dollar a day."

Jack nodded, pulled his leather pouch from his pocket, and extracted a double eagle, a half eagle, and a silver dollar from the pouch. He stacked the three coins on the desk and dropped the pouch back into his vest.

Blake wiped the coins from the desk into his hand, opened a drawer, and dropped them into separate compartments. He retrieved a receipt book and quickly wrote a receipt for Jack and handed it to him. "Thank you, sir. If you find yourself needing anything, just let me know. Should you want to clean up, we do have tubs in back, but I'd recommend Mr. Wickham's place, across the street. He runs a bathhouse and a barbershop, besides being the dentist and undertaker. Dusty, a friend of mine, works for him, keeps the water hot. They've got nice showers. I use them every once in a while myself, only a dime a shower."

Marsden nodded his agreement. "I've been known to use them too, especially after working in my mine. Those are fine showers, plenty of hot water. He's also got shaving gear, keeps his razors sharp. Got soap too."

Jack grinned at the thought of a shower. His dust-covered body had gotten soaked in the rain after escaping the Apaches on his ride from Las Cruces. He was a mess. He needed a shave and a shower and a haircut. He also needed his clothes cleaned. Addressing the clerk, he asked, "What's your name?"

"My name is Blake Colson, Mr. Sage. The night clerk is an older gentleman. His name is Emmett Sands. He lives in the hotel. In fact, his room is right next to yours, number eight. You're number six, upstairs and on the right side, about halfway down the hall." He handed Jack his key. It was attached to a brass medallion with the number 6 on it.

Jack took it with his left hand. "Thanks, Blake. After I drop my things, I think I'll wander over to Mr. Wickham's establishment." He turned to Hank Marsden, a lopsided grin on his face. "Thanks for the conversation and warning. I'll stay on the lookout for any and all desperadoes."

Marsden shook his head. "I know you're funning me, but mark my words. There'll be men hunting you, and it can happen anytime. You'd best be on the lookout."

Jack extended his hand. "Seriously, Hank, thanks. I'll keep a sharp eye out. I'd like to get with you again and talk about the gold strikes around here. I've got a bit of the bug, and I'm anxious to take a look around. Any suggestions would be a great help since this is the first time I've ever prospected."

Marsden broke into a wide grin. "Now you're talking about something that is dear to my heart. Sure, I'll tell you all I know. What about tonight? We can get together for a bite, and I'll go over equipment you might consider buying, and what you should be looking for. How does that sound?"

Blake cleared his throat, and both men turned to look at him. "Mr. Marsden, you were having dinner with us tonight."

"Yes, yes, of course. I'm sure Wanda wouldn't mind an additional guest. What do you think?"

Jack shook his head. "I can't impose. Hank, we can get together tomorrow, before I pull out."

It was Blake's turn to speak up. "Mr. Sage, Wanda would love to meet you. You're the talk of the town today, saving Judge Coleman and chasing off Rush's bunch. She'd be thrilled to have you over for dinner. Please, you won't be an imposition at all."

Jack looked at Marsden, who backed up his son-in-law's statement. "My daughter loves people. Come on. Plus, she's a great cook. She learned on me after her mother died."

"In that case, I'd be obliged. What time?"

Blake hurried from behind the counter. "Five thirty would be perfect." He picked up a bowler hat from under the counter and slipped it on, stepping to Hank. "Could you watch the counter for me? It'll just be a minute. I'm going to run home and tell Wanda. I'll be right back."

Marsden smiled at the excited young man. "Sure thing, Blake. Get going, but don't be too long. I've got to get to the mine."

"I'll be back before you know it." Blake dashed through the open door of the hotel and disappeared down the street.

Through the large glass window, Jack watched the young man trot carefully along the side of the street, where the mud was beginning to dry. "Thanks, Hank. I need to take these things to my room before I head to the barber. See you this evening, and I warn you, I'm going to pick your brain."

IN CLEAN CLOTHES, Jack relaxed into the barber's chair. He felt five pounds lighter after washing the dirt and mud from his body. Dusty had been a big help, keeping the hot water flowing while he showered, and taking his dirty clothes to the Chinese laundry. He had assured him the clothes would be waiting for him in his room when he got back from his search for gold.

Search for gold, Jack thought, *isn't that a hoot. Who would have ever thought I'd be a prospector? I've worn a lot of hats, but this is a first.* He was looking forward to talking to Marsden about finding and recognizing gold. Jack closed his eyes while Wickham cut his hair and talked. His mind wandered as he relaxed. *My money's running low from the cattle drive to Ellsworth, Kansas. I know my finding gold is a long shot, but I've been lucky before, why not now? Gold. The word itself has a ring to it. Do I have the fever? I have to admit I'm a little excited about searching, but I don't know if I'd recognize it if I saw it.*

Wickham droned on about the shooting in the courtroom

and Rush's dead gunman. Jack's mind drifted back to the court-room. *I cannot believe Rush had the gall to charge into a federal court-room, pistol-whip Marshal Hardwick, and take his kid.* He could feel his anger rising. *If he hadn't taken him from the court, I wouldn't have had to shoot him. Now with Hardwick down, am I doing the right thing? Should I take the job as deputy U.S. Marshal?*

He let out a long sigh. *Sometimes you have to think of yourself. I'll take a couple of weeks, maybe a month. If I don't find anything, and if Hardwick still needs me, I'll sign on with him. What difference can two weeks or a month make? Maybe I'll go see Hardwick before supper tonight, just to see how he's doing.*

Jack, always cautious, though he hadn't let on, had been listening closely as Hank Marsden issued his warning about Rush. He shifted the .36-caliber Remington New Model Police revolver he held loosely in his left hand under the barber cloth to a more comfortable position and stretched his long legs in front of him. The hammer was eared back, and his finger lay relaxed outside the trigger guard.

The smell of the barbershop, mortuary, dental office, whatever it was, was not bad. He had figured the smell of death would be over-powering. Jasper Rush and the gunman Taggert, who had died from Jack's gunshots, lay less than twenty feet toward the back of the shot-gun-style building. They were stacked on a table with a sheet over them, waiting for Wickham to bury them. However, the barber's colognes and lotions did a good job of covering the other odors.

Jack grew more drowsy as Wickham droned on.

The door opened, jingling the bell hanging above the door-frame. Moments later, boots and spurs echoed on the barber-shop's planks. Wickham's scissors stopped clicking. "See here, boys. I don't want any trouble in here. Mr. Sage is a customer."

Jack cracked an eyelid.

Three men had walked into Wickham's establishment. The leader was short, skinny, young, pimply-faced, and cocky. He spoke up, his voice a high-pitched drawl. "We ain't after any trouble, Wickham. We just rode in and want you to show us our friend Taggert, who, if I ain't missing my guess, this here feller killed."

Jack lazily opened one eye. "Mr. Wickham is busy, boys. He'll be done shortly. Why don't you have a seat." Jack nodded at the four chairs against the wall of the barbershop portion of Wickham's establishment.

The three men began to move away from the door, and instead of sitting, they began to spread out, facing Jack and Wickham.

One of the other men passed behind the cocky one and continued to the man's right.

Jack's voice changed from friendly to commanding. "That's far enough. Your options have changed. Turn around and head out the door."

The three men stopped, and the oldest spoke up, nodding to the kid. "You must not know who this is, mister. This here is Chance Cooper, the Gila Kid."

The kid had gone into a crouch, an evil grin splitting his face. "I've already killed a passel of people, old feller. I don't mind adding you to the list."

Old feller, Jack thought, *first time I've been called that, and here I've yet to pass my thirty-eighth birthday.* His face broke into a cold smile. "Sonny, you'd best be careful, or this chance will be your last chance, Chancy." He watched the grin disappear from the kid's face, replaced by a scowl. Jack supposed this was the kid's idea of a threatening stare, but it didn't do much for him. Even so, he didn't want this deteriorating into a gunfight inside Wickham's shop. Everyone would end up getting shot, including the proprietor. Using his right hand, he slowly lifted the barber cloth from across his body, exposing the Remington in his left hand, hammer back and finger on the trigger.

The trio's eyes grew big, including Cooper's. Jack slowly began to stand.

He could see the surprise and fear in the eyes of the two men accompanying Cooper, but the kid's face was cold, completely fearless, and angry.

The little gunman slowly moved his hand away from his revolver, his eyes locked on Jack's Remington. "I don't like you calling me sonny. It ain't respectful."

"When you do something worthy of respect, I imagine you'll get it. Now do like I said, and hit the trail. Mr. Wickham needs to finish my haircut."

The other two men began to move, but Cooper remained stationary. Jack could see the gunfighter didn't like the idea of backing down, which showed just how unseasoned he was. A man with experience would have been thankful for the second chance and would've eased on out from under the gun. He wouldn't have been frightened, just prudent, planning for the next engagement. Not this kid. His pride was hurt, and he wanted it mended.

"Don't make a bad choice, Cooper. You'll be dead before you can get your hand on your Colt. All you'll manage to do is get your friends shot. Use your head."

The big fella who had introduced the gunfighter fidgeted and raised his hands high enough so that it was obvious to Jack he wasn't planning on drawing. The other man had slid his hands into the armholes of his vest, also making the same statement.

"Cooper, how much money do you have on you?"

The kid said, "I don't know, why?"

"I just want to make sure there's enough for Mr. Wickham here to bury you." Jack kept his eyes on the gunman. "Mr. Wickham, how much do you charge for a burial?"

Wickham's voice quivered slightly. "Ten dollars to be wrapped in a sheet and dropped in a hole on boot hill. Twenty-five for a pine box and a preacher to speak over you."

"Hear that, Cooper? It'll cost you twenty-five for a nice burial. You have twenty-five on you? You're going to need it. Because if you don't start moving right now, I'm dropping you where you stand. I'm tired of waiting for my haircut."

Cooper straightened further, licked his lips, made a decision, and sidled toward the door. Reaching it, he placed his hand on the latch and turned to Jack. "I'll meet you in the street when you've finished with your haircut. Make it a good one. It'll be your last." He turned and marched out the door, his two companions following.

The door closed, and Wickham said, "What're you gonna do, Mr. Sage? They'll kill you."

"First, I'm going to finish my haircut. Then I'll worry about Cooper. What can you tell me about him? I've never heard of the Gila Kid."

Jack relaxed back into the chair, and Wickham spread the barber cloth across his body, fastening it at his neck. "He showed up maybe two months ago. He's killed two men here in Silver City since he arrived. The kid's greased lightning with that gun. He doesn't mind who he shoots, and he's got a short temper, goes off at anything."

"He works for Rush?"

"Yeah. He's really attached himself to Rush. It's almost as if he sees Rush as the father he never had. You mess with Rush, you're messin' with the Gila Kid." Wickham continued to work in silence.

"Why hasn't the sheriff or one of his deputies or Marshal Hardwick arrested him?"

Wickham's scissors stopped, and he walked around in front of Jack so he could look directly at him. "I don't know for sure, but I think the Kid has them buffaloed. Now, I'm not meaning Marshal Hardwick. He's tougher than old boot leather. I heard he was planning on arresting the kid, afore he got pistol-whipped.

Gettin' slammed in the head from Rush may change the situation."

Wickham stepped back behind Jack and continued to work in silence, and Jack thought, *Rush and his gunfighters really do have their way around here. I'd better check on Hardwick before I commit to prospecting. Dang it, I want to go find gold.*

Wickham finished with the haircut and swept Jack's thick brown hair, a few gray streaks beginning to appear, back with his comb. He splashed a little of his sweet-smelling cologne in his hands and patted Jack's neck and cheeks. With a flourish, he swept the barber cloth from the big man. "That'll be fifteen cents, Mr. Sage."

Jack stood, dropped the revolver back into its holster, and paid Wickham. He could see Cooper standing across the street, leaning against a hitching rail, but he couldn't see the other two men who had been with him. "Doc's office next door?"

"Yes, sir, right next door."

"Does it have a back door?"

"It sure does. Just go out back, past my shower lean-to, and turn left. It'll be the first door you come to."

"Thanks. Was I you, I wouldn't be heading out your front door anytime soon. My guess is there's at least one rifle and maybe two aimed at it."

Wickham looked at Jack, then at his front door, and back to Jack. "I sure won't. No, sir, I sure won't go out there."

Jack nodded to the man, grabbed his hat from the rack, leveled it on his head, and strode past the corpses to the back of the building. Passing the showers, he turned left and within three steps was at the doc's back door. He knocked twice and waited. He was about to knock again when the door swung open. It was Martha Pratt, the doctor's wife.

She smiled. "Why, Mr. Sage, we don't usually receive guests or patients at the back door, but do come in." She glanced up at the door facing, her smile widening. "You should duck, or you might need to see my husband."

Jack grinned back at her as he removed his hat, ducked to lower his tall frame, and stepped through the door. "Sorry to bother you, ma'am, but is Marshal Hardwick awake?"

"Oh, yes, he's in the parlor with my husband and Judge Coleman." She motioned down the hallway. "Would you like a cup of coffee?"

Jack was never one to pass up a home-brewed cup of coffee. "Yes, ma'am. That'd be mighty nice."

"Well, you go on in and join them, and I'll bring you one."

"Thanks, ma'am." Jack turned and walked down the hallway. It opened into the parlor. Marshal Hardwick, his head and cheek bandaged, and Judge Coleman were each sitting in green wing-back chairs, a side table between them. Dr. Pratt was sitting at the end of a long green couch with thick hand-carved mahogany armrests. A rich brown mahogany coffee table sat in front of him.

Dr. Pratt rose. "Come in, Mr. Sage. This is a pleasant surprise, since you were the subject of our conversation."

"Really." Jack nodded at Judge Coleman and spoke to Marshal Hardwick. "We didn't get a chance to meet. I'm Jack Sage. I just came by to see how you're doing."

Hardwick rose, unsteady, and extended his hand. "Good to meet you. Saw you in El Paso when you were chasing those child-stealers. Understand you caught 'em all."

Mrs. Pratt, carrying a cup of coffee, came into the parlor, and the judge rose. "Please sit down, Judge. Mr. Sage, here is your coffee." She set the cup down on the coffee table in front of the couch.

"I'm much obliged, ma'am."

Martha Pratt addressed her husband. "David, I'm going to the back. If anyone needs anything else, please call me."

"Thank you, honey."

She turned and was gone from the room. Jack stepped past the coffee table to the couch, sat, and picked up the sugar spoon. Spooning sugar into his cup, he said, "You were talking about me?"

The judge cleared his throat. "Yes, Jack, we were discussing our need for you in the Marshal Service."

Jack poured cream into his cup, picked up his spoon, and stirred the sugar and cream into the coffee. He took a sip of the sweet concoction and looked at the marshal. "How are you feeling?"

The marshal gave a single nod and locked his pale gray eyes on Jack. "I'm fine. What's wrong with you? Why won't you join us?"

5

J ack stared back at the marshal. He could feel his temper rising. The thought ran through his mind, *Those eyes may look like chips from a block of ice, and I bet he's used them on many an occasion to intimidate a lawbreaker, but they don't intimidate me.* "I'll tell you, Marshal. I plan on doing a little prospecting. That's why I headed up here in the first place. My finances are getting a little low, so I'd like to replenish them. Not that it's any of your business."

Jack, seeing the marshal tense at his comment, turned to the doctor. "Dr. Pratt, how about telling me the marshal's true condition? I saw him wobble when he stood."

Pratt glanced at Judge Coleman and then at Marshal Hardwick.

The marshal glared at Pratt. "I said I'm doing fine. Anyway, Sage, like you said, it's none of your business."

The judge nodded to the doctor. Pratt cleared his throat. "Well, he's not really doing fine. He has a concussion. When he stands, he suffers from nausea, dizziness, and instability. My recommendation is that he do no marshaling or horseback riding, and use a cane, until those symptoms disappear."

Hardwick glared at the doctor, but said nothing.

Judge Coleman leaned forward in his chair. "Jack, you see why we need your help. Rush needs to be brought in for many reasons. He attempted to abscond with his son, and he assaulted and shot up the court. He and his men wounded several of Silver City's citizens. I could go on, but the bottom line is I need you to join the Marshal Service. It'll be only until we clean up this Silver City mess. When that's done and Marshal Hardwick is back on his feet, you're free to resign, leave, prospect, whatever you want to do. But you're needed now."

Jack took another sip of his coffee, set the cup down, and leaned back into the soft couch. The last thing he wanted to do was get embroiled in a local problem. It was time he looked out for himself, but someone needed to put a halt to Rush's free rein. Silent, he took another sip. Finally he spoke. "I had a run-in with a pimply-faced runt calls himself the Gila Kid."

Hardwick straightened. "What happened?"

Jack explained what had happened at the barbershop.

Hardwick was unable to keep a tight grin off his face. "Guess they were surprised."

"You might say that, but the kid wasn't very happy about having to back down. There for a few seconds, I thought he was going to draw with me holding an aimed and cocked revolver on him. He's outside waiting for me right now."

Hardwick turned his ice-gray eyes on Jack. "The kid's crazy, cold as a fish. You planning on meeting him, or do you want my help?"

Jack shook his head. "No, I don't want your help. I just wanted to make sure the law wasn't going to be after me if I end up having to kill this kid. He's making it mighty difficult to keep from it."

Hardwick gave a short hard laugh. "Cooper's fast. You'd better think twice unless you are very, very good. He's young and has quick reflexes. Supposedly he's killed seven or eight men in stand-up fights. No telling how many we haven't heard about."

Judge Coleman leaned forward. "Marshal Hardwick was going to arrest him, before . . ." The judge looked at the marshal, hesitated, and then continued, "Anyway, join the service. Go out there with the law backing you. If you don't have to kill him, you can throw him in jail. Without this, it'll just be another gunfight." He pulled a badge from his pocket and tossed it across the room to Jack. "I'll swear you in right now. Then you'll be representing the law when you meet the kid."

Jack looked at the badge, rubbing the writing with his thumb. Turning it over, he noticed a stain on the back. He recognized it for what it was, old blood, no longer red. He looked up at Coleman.

"That's Chet Weaver's badge. The marshal Cooper killed. Figured you wouldn't mind having it to remind you of the value of the law."

Jack didn't much like the judge. He was pompous and full of himself, but to be honest, he hadn't liked many judges, and he did believe in the law. If this country was going to become civilized and be safe for the average law-abiding citizen, it would need the judges and the laws, but dang it, he wanted to be gold prospecting. He held the judge's stare for a few moments longer. "Alright, I'll do it. I don't especially like the idea, but I'll do it. You'd best understand, though, when this is cleaned up, I'm hunting gold, not men. Is that clear?"

Both the marshal and the judge nodded. The judge said, "Stand up and raise your right hand."

Jack followed the command.

"Do you swear to uphold the law to the best of your ability?"

"Yep."

"Then pin it on. You are now a Deputy U.S. Marshal. I'll take care of the paperwork and get you a copy. You now represent the United States government."

"And you work for me," Marshal Hardwick said. "You'll do what I say and conduct yourself in the manner you're told. Is that clear?"

Jack was still standing. He turned to Hardwick. "You listen to me, and listen close. This badge may say deputy, but I work for the judge. He hired me, and he swore me in." Jack watched the jaw muscles of Hardwick clinch.

Hardwick was about to speak, but the judge shoved a hand in front of him and addressed Jack. "Right now, your job is to get Cooper and his accomplices arrested, and if they're still breathing when you're done, you're to throw them in jail."

Hardwick, his eyebrows pulled together and his lips pursed, leaned back in his chair, placed his forearms on the armrests, and unclinched his fists. "You said he had two men with him?"

Jack nodded.

"Then they'll be waiting to ambush you. The Rush bunch hang out at the Golden Nugget saloon. It's across the street and a couple of buildings north. I'm bettin' they'll both be at windows upstairs." He turned to Dr. Pratt. "Doc, would you mind headin' over to the sheriff's office and roust out those deputies? Tell 'em to go check upstairs in the Nugget. If those two are settin' up an ambush, the deputies are to arrest them and wait until Sage comes out of the alley next to your office. When they see him, give him a wave, then take the rats to jail. If they're not there, locate them and let Sage know. Can you do that?"

The doctor was already standing. "Of course I can." He pulled his coat on, placed his small, dark gray Stetson on his head, and called, "I'll be right back, Martha." Before she could answer, he was gone.

Jack pinned the badge on his black and gray striped vest, just above the upper left pocket, and sat back down on the couch. Martha Pratt stepped into the room, and all three men began to rise.

"Please, gentlemen, keep your seats. Where is David going?"

The judge explained. Her brow wrinkled, and her full lips drew tight. Saying nothing, she turned and departed to the back.

Jack had barely relaxed into the comfortable couch when the doctor came through the front door. "That was simple. They were headed to the undertaker's place to take a look at Rush's and Taggert's bodies. I caught them just as they were going in. They're headed over to the Nugget right now. Cooper is still across the street waiting."

Jack stood. "Guess there's no time like the present. I'll ease out the back. If your hunch is right, business is going to pick up mighty quick."

The judge rose. "Thanks for taking the job, and good luck to you. Be careful. The marshal is right. The kid is fast, but if you can, try to take him alive. Give him a chance to surrender."

"I always do, Judge. It'll be up to him." Jack walked through the hallway into the kitchen.

Martha Pratt was standing at the counter, cutting onions. There were tears in her eyes. She looked up at Jack and gave him a small smile. "I always cry when I cut onions."

He nodded. "Yes, ma'am, so do I. Thanks for the hospitality and the coffee. It was mighty good." He ducked his head, stepped through the back door, and straightened, putting his hat on and adjusting it. He pulled his watch from an inside vest pocket, his thumb drifting over the emerald set into the top of the pocket watch. It was shaped like an exploding grenade, the symbol of the French Foreign Legion, and had been given to him by his wife. His mind drifted to Yasmina, his beautiful young Algerian wife, and his baby son, gone so many years before.

He forced the thoughts away and stepped around the back corner of the building, into the alley. The mud was drying fast. *This time tomorrow, these streets will be hard-packed and dusty,* he thought. Jack moved rapidly along the length of the alley to the edge of the street. He spotted the Nugget saloon, and his eyes moved to the upstairs windows. There was only one deputy, holding one of the men who had been with Cooper. The deputy shook his head, holding up one finger. *I'm glad they got one of them,* he thought. He began examining every window, doorway, and alley on the other side of the street. Once he had visually cleared all the openings that could provide cover to a bushwhacker, he stepped out from the corner of the building and started down the street toward Cooper, staying close to the buildings' fronts. If the other man was on this side, he would have a tough time getting a shot at him without exposing himself. He watched Cooper while remaining alert to any other threatening movement as he walked.

Cooper straightened at the sight of Jack. The boy gave him a confident grin. *Like a hungry wolf,* Jack thought. Jack's breathing slowed, and he could feel his heart rate dropping. He took deliberate deep breaths. He had learned the method when he was young and in the Legion. A man could control his emotions. It took practice, but he could learn to be calm and cool no matter how tough the situation. Nearing the gunfighter, a slow grin coursed Jack's wide face. His white teeth glistened. He could see Cooper's grin turn to a frown. Jack stopped when he was directly across the wide street from Cooper, a long shot for a handgun, especially fired from a fast draw. This was in his favor. His grin widened.

Jack had been in situations like this before and was well aware the fastest gun didn't always win. There was a chance he might be hit, but if he drew, his first shot had to be accurate. He made a critical decision. Normally, he was closer and would draw and fire from the hip. But this was a different situation. He was farther away, and there was a good chance the kid would miss at this distance. Jack would draw quickly, bring the weapon up in a dueling stance, and aim. It was the only way to be sure of a hit.

Cooper yelled, "What are you grinning at, man? Are you crazy? And what's that badge you're wearing?"

Jack opened his mouth to answer, but a large, longhaired,

brown mutt, his tail tucked between his legs, raced from the alleyway to Jack's left, turned and began barking at something in the alley. *Thank you, pup,* he thought. *At least I have an idea where the second man is located. Hopefully the other deputy will take care of him.*

"Shut up, dog!" Cooper yelled. "If you ain't quiet, I'll take care of you when I finish with this lawman."

The dog continued to bark.

Jack watched the kid. He was excited, shifting his weight from one foot to the other. That was good. His adrenaline would be flowing. He'd be faster but less accurate. "Cooper, you should think real hard about what you're about to do. First, you're not going to kill me, but let's say you hit me. I've just been sworn in as a deputy marshal. If you kill me, you'll be hunted for the remainder of your life until you are arrested, tried, and hanged. So this is a situation where if you beat me, you lose. If you're smart, and I think you are, you'll surrender to me. I'll take you to jail, and you'll only be tried for threatening an officer of the court. Think about that. A while in jail versus a bullet or a rope. Seems like an easy choice to me."

Of a sudden, Jack heard the sound of something heavy striking flesh, immediately followed by the thunk of a body collapsing to the ground. One of the deputies stepped from the alley and held a thumb up. Jack's grin got wider. "Listen to me, Cooper. We've gotten your man in the Nugget and this one in the alley. It's just you and me now. It should be an easy choice for you. Why don't you drop those guns and make the smart move."

Cooper's gaze cut to the Nugget and back to Jack. "It's time you made a decision, Cooper."

The Gila Kid took a step forward, and the mud sucked at his boot. "Come on over here, Sage. What's the matter, you scared to get close?"

"Of course I am, Cooper. I don't want to die any more than you do. All you know about me is that I'm big. You have to figure I

can absorb a lot of lead, and you're right. I've done it before. I
don't like it, but I know I can. I promise you, if you draw, you'll
die. Even if you hit me, I'll kill you, boy, and that's not something
I want to do. Think of all the girls you haven't met yet, the places
you haven't seen. Drop those guns and make it easy on both
of us."

Jack watched the tip of the boy's tongue flick out and lick his
lips. The thought flashed, *He's gonna do it. That crazy kid.*

Cooper dropped into a crouch, his hand hovering over his
gun butt. "You talk too much, old man. Why don't you just go to
the devil."

Jack watched the Gila Kid's hand flash, and saw the weapon
rising from his holster. Automatically, Jack's Remington was also
moving, gripped in his right hand. He had done this thousands of
times both in practice and facing another gun. There was no
thought in it. His mind was elsewhere, processing the Kid's speed.
He was fast, but not as fast as Jack. Unfortunately, today Jack's
weapon had to travel a farther distance before it fired, and
though he was quick, as was his aiming eye, it would be slower
than the Kid's shot from the hip.

He brought the weapon to bear. The front and rear sight came
into alignment with the Kid's chest. He heard the Kid's weapon
fire, and saw the flash. His eyes even momentarily registered the
dark ball speeding out of the smoke cloud around the muzzle of
the boy's revolver. He squeezed the trigger.

Expecting the jar and shock of a bullet striking his flesh, he
was surprised at the sound of glass breaking and falling to the
street behind him. By this time, his hammer was back again, his
smoke cloud had cleared, and his sights were aligning, unneces-
sarily. He no longer had a standing target. The Kid, earlier
anxious to kill Jack and feeling invincible, was kneeling in the
muddy street, holding his upper chest with both hands. Blood
flowed through his fingers, turning them bright red, while his
blue eyes were locked on Jack, staring in shock and fright.

The doctor, with his bag, was racing from his office. Jack lowered his .36-caliber Remington Police and started across the street, his weapon in his hand and ready. The Kid's eyes, wide and horrified at what had happened, followed him as he approached.

The river down the middle of the street was gone, but the surface was still muddy. He slogged across, keeping his eyes locked on Cooper. There had been many a man killed by a shot and wounded, or dying, opponent. The Kid's eyes never left him.

"You shot me." His voice was filled with surprise.

Jack looked down on the boy. He looked even smaller lying crumpled in the street. "That's what happens in gunfights. One or maybe both get shot. How does it feel?"

Jack could see Cooper was fighting to hold back the tears, but they were slowly running from the corners of his blue eyes, coursing their way through the boy's pimples.

The Kid gritted out, "It hurts like the dickens. Am I dying?"

"Think about it. What you're feeling is the same thing the men you shot felt." Jack, relenting somewhat, said, "Doc?"

The doctor looked up from his kneeling position over the Kid, where he had laid the boy, still in the mud. He shook his head. "You missed. You hit him just above his right lung. If he doesn't get an infection, he'll live."

Jack, still staring down at the boy, gave him a slow wink and shoved his revolver back into its holster. "I never miss, not from that firing position. Remember the pain and the fear, boy. If you're lucky, you'll be getting a second chance. Use it proper."

"Doc, you want him taken to your place, or can you care for him in the jail?"

The doctor leaned back and placed his hands on his thighs. "It'd be better if he was brought to my office. Martha and I can look after him until he's feeling well enough to be moved." He looked at one of the deputies. "I'll let you know when you can have him."

The deputy nodded. "Sounds good to me, Doc. Rush ain't

gonna be too happy when he hears about this. In one day his son gets killed and the Kid loses a gunfight to the same man who killed his son." The deputy looked at Jack and shook his head. "He ain't gonna be happy even one little bit."

Jack saw Martha bring a folded stretcher from their house, speak to a man, and give it to him. The man slogged across the street. "Doc, yore wife sent me with this here stretcher for the Kid. She said to tell you she has your office ready when you need it."

"Thanks, Bill." He looked around the crowd and pointed at two hefty young men. "Stanley, you and Mathew bring the stretcher over here, and let's get this boy on it."

The two took the stretcher from Bill, opened it, and held it low while the deputies lifted Cooper. The gunfighter gritted his teeth in an obvious attempt to keep from crying out, but a deep groan escaped, his youthful face etched with pain. His eyes again found Jack. His voice, still high-pitched, was weaker and hesitant between winces of pain. "You could have killed me?"

"I've been doing this a lot of years, boy. Like I said, from that stance? I don't miss. Yeah, I could've killed you. I could've just as easily put that bullet right between those blue eyes, but I was hoping there still might be a little good in that hard young heart of yours." Jack paused, his face hardening. "But if there's a next time, I'll not miss."

6

The doc motioned to the boys, and they started toward his office with Cooper. The little gunman held Jack's gaze as he bounced across the street until finally disappearing behind the door.

The crowd began to disperse, and Jack felt a hand on his shoulder. He turned to see the judge standing next to him. "That was an intentional shot?"

Jack nodded.

The judge looked across the street to where Jack had been standing. "You've got quite a way with a pistol."

"It'll do."

"You think he'll change his ways?"

"I have no idea, Judge. He's got some pain to live through and time to think about it. Maybe adding a close brush with death might turn him around, and it might not. Most gunslingers feel like they're invincible until they get shot the first time. That's usually when reality sets in. We'll just have to give him time and see if he makes a change, but I've got work to do now."

"Are you heading after Rush?"

"Nope, not today. There's been enough excitement for me. I've got a supper engagement with Hank Marsden, his daughter, and his son-in-law." He pulled out his pocket watch and checked the time. It was fifteen minutes after five. "I'd best be on my way. Can you tell me where Blake Colson and his wife live?"

Jack saw Coleman eyeing his watch. "I can, if you'll tell me about that fine watch. That looks like an emerald set in the top."

"It is." He closed the watch and slid it back into his pocket. "It was given to me many years ago."

The judge watched Jack's face as he spoke. "Yes, I think there is quite a story to go along with it. I'd love to hear it."

"One of these days, maybe. Now, the Colsons'?"

Coleman nodded. "Ah, yes, of course." He pointed north. "Up the street and just past the Nugget. There's a cross street with a few small homes on it. Turn west, and it'll be the fourth house on the right. You can't miss it. Mrs. Colson likes blue."

Jack nodded his thanks and started off.

The judge called, "See me before you leave."

Jack raised a hand in acknowledgment and kept walking. He was looking forward to a fine meal and learning about gold prospecting. There had been nothing mentioned indicating he couldn't mix his search for Rush with a little prospecting. Passing the Golden Nugget, he glanced inside. Everything looked normal. The thought ran through his mind, *But when does that ever mean anything?*

Reaching the narrow cross street, he turned left. Several houses along the street were painted a sedate white, a couple were only whitewashed, but one, fourth up the street on the right side, stood out like an early mountain lupine in a late snow.

The blue was soft and inviting. *Almost calming,* Jack thought. *Calm would be a great way to end this day, plus learning a little about gold from Hank.*

∼

No more than twenty yards to his right, tall pines thrust to the sky, thrashing like weeds from the heightening wind. He pulled his jacket closer. The north wind moaned through the trees. Limbs rattled, hammering against other branches and trunks. Occasionally, dead or diseased, one would crash to the forest floor. Leaving Silver City this morning, the wind had been blowing, but had been warm, out of the southeast and nowhere near as strong. Through the morning it had gradually shifted from southeast to southwest and increased until now it was gusting with fierce determination and had moved into the northwest, nearing gale force. Clouds raced across the sky, and the temperature felt like it was plummeting like a stone.

Jack patted Thunder, his big gray, on the neck. "Looks like I picked the wrong day to take after Rush, boy. We're liable to get a little chilly tonight if the falling branches and trees don't kill us first." The big horse, normally calm in almost any situation, was jumpy. His head was up, and his ears twitched toward every crack or crash of a tree.

Boulders, some as big as a house, looked like they had been dropped from a giant's marbles bag, haphazardly scattering along the cliff. Near and to the right, tall pines thrashed against one another. To their left, the cliff fell away into a narrow canyon several hundred feet deep. A ribbon of water raced along the distant bottom, and across the canyon, the pines continued in a jagged green vista. Jack's eyes scanned into the canyon, his mind drifting to his supper with Hank and the newlyweds.

Not only had the successful prospector taught him a great deal about gold, what it looked like, where to find it, and fool's gold, iron pyrite, at supper last night, but he had given Jack solid directions to Rush's ranch. There were few other people who actually knew the location of the Three Sixes. Hank had just happened upon it when he was prospecting, long before he struck it big. He'd been smart enough to restrain his urge to ride in until he figured out who owned it, surprised to find a ranch headquarters so remotely located in Apache country.

He had lain on the hillside, watching the ranch activity, for well over an hour. Just before he was about to crawl away from the ridge, Rush and two of his boys had come out of the house. Hank had said he immediately identified the burly father. They spoke momentarily, and the two boys headed for the barn. That was when he figured it was time for him to haul his freight out of there.

I agree with Hank, Jack thought. *I'd like to know what Rush is up to—*

The loop of a lasso settled over Jack's shoulders, dropping to his waist and yanking tight, locking his arms at his sides. Before the first rope had pulled tight, a second loop found him. There was a solid yank, and he felt himself flying from Thunder's back. He struck the rocky ground with such force the air was knocked from him, along with his hat.

He was dazed. As if through a fog, dull and distant voices, whoops, and yells sounded. He heard a strident voice roar, "Get that horse," and then he faded out.

He was jerked back to consciousness. Jack was rolling and scraping across the rocky ground behind two racing horses. His body slammed against a huge boulder, then lurched away. He felt something smash into his ribs. He tensed his neck, pulling his head in against his chest, trying to protect it.

The dragging must have been short. The horses stopped, and Jack struggled to his feet. In front of him sat Rush on a big red bay, and five of his men alongside him. Two of them held the ends of the ropes. Jack started to shrug out of the ropes, and the two riders yanked them tight again.

Rush laughed. "Keep him tight, boys. I've got plans for this big feller." He leaned forward, resting his forearms on his saddle horn, and glared at Jack. "How're you doing, mister gunfighter?"

Jack, almost as angry with himself as he was with Rush,

returned the glare. "Get these ropes off me, Rush. You're in deep enough trouble without making things worse." He looked at the other men, pausing to make eye contact with each. "That goes for you men as well. I'm a deputy United States Marshal, and I've been sent to bring your boss in for trial. You don't want to be interfering with me."

Rush threw back his head and roared with laughter. His men joined in.

"Have you ever heard the like, Pa? Now that takes gall to stand there with our ropes on him and claim he's gonna take you to jail."

Elijah Rush turned to his right and addressed the man who had spoken. "Boone, boy, didn't you hear him? He's a *U-nited* States Marshal. That makes him a big man in his own eyes." He turned back to Jack. "Where's your badge, big man? Ain't you supposed to be wearing your badge?"

"My badge is on my vest, under my coat, where it belongs. You've had your fun, Rush. Get these ropes off me. Don't get your son involved in this. Give up. Turn yourself over to me, and I promise you a fair trial. None of the citizens you shot have died. You won't be facing a murder charge."

Rush leaned further toward Jack, his face grim with hate. "I don't give a hang about those folks in town. They could've all died, makes no never mind to me. What I care about is having the man who killed my son standing right here in front of me."

A younger fella to Rush's left yelled, "Hang him, Pa. You said it. He killed Jasper. He deserves to die. Hang him hard. Make him suffer."

Jack knew what hang him hard meant. When a man was hanged in such a manner, a hangman's noose, the knotting of which normally broke a man's neck when he was dropped or yanked from a horse, was not used. Rather, the rope formed only a loop, causing the man to choke to death, his body screaming for air. He didn't hanker after either.

Rush grinned at Jack. "Reckon you haven't met my boys. This one to my left, excited to see yore neck stretched, is my youngest son, Vern. He can be a little bloody, kinda like his poor, deceased twin brother." His voice hardened. "That would be the innocent boy you shot in the head, lawman. His name was Jasper." Relaxing again, he straightened in the saddle and angled his head to the right. "This here is Boone. He's a good boy. Like those two cowhands holding your ropes, he'll do most whatever I tell him."

Jack said nothing. He could see there would be no persuading these men to release him. The sharp wind blew through his black hair. *This is not looking good,* he thought. *At least I still have my guns. With enough slack from these ropes, I might reach them.* His eyes hadn't left Elijah Rush's face.

As if reading his mind, Rush said, "You boys keep those ropes tight. We don't want him getting to either one of them guns. I've seen what he can do with 'em."

Jack felt the ropes tighten around his body, pulling in opposite directions. He stutter-stepped to prevent falling, moving back and forth until the pressure of the ropes evened out.

"You boys getting cold?" Rush asked, then answered his own question. "I am. We still have a ride back to the ranch. Let's take him on over to the hangin' tree. It's not like we haven't used it before."

Vern was almost bouncing in the saddle with excitement. "Yeah, Pa. Hang him. I say hang him. Give him a taste of the rope."

Before he turned his horse, Elijah Rush reached over and patted his son on the shoulder. "Relax, boy. That's what we're gonna do. We're gonna find out just how far that marshal's neck will stretch."

They moved out in the direction Jack had originally been traveling. He hustled along behind, attempting to keep enough slack in the ropes so he could maintain his footing. If he fell, he knew they wouldn't stop. They'd drag him all the way to the tree they were talking about. His back was already bleeding from the short drag he had earlier endured. No telling how long this one would be, and all it would take was a single strike against one of the rocks or boulders with his head, and he'd be long gone, no longer worrying about the cold.

He wasn't able to judge the distance they had traveled. The blow to his head, when he had been yanked off Thunder, had muddled his thinking. *Thunder,* he thought, *what has happened to you?* He looked around. No one was leading the horse. His big gray must have made it to the trees before they could get a loop over his neck. *I sure hope you've headed back to town, boy.*

They halted.

Jack's eyes sought and found the skeleton of a big tree. It was old, barren of leaves, and sat on the edge of the canyon. In fact, some of the naked branches thrust out above the canyon wall and the river below. One, a particularly heavy branch, extended near, but not over the canyon's edge. The tree, though old, looked strong, especially the limb from which they were about to hang him. *Seasoned is the word,* he thought.

Elijah Rush turned to his youngest son. "Vern, git down, boy. Go get that feller's guns. I don't want him gettin' a lucky shot off."

The boy leaped from the horse and ran over to Jack. He unbuckled his gun belt and yanked it from around his waist. Jack watched the kid drop his belt, with his guns and knife, in the dirt, and gritted his teeth. Vern switched his attention to Jack's pockets, starting with his coat.

"Leave him be, boy. There'll be plenty of time for that after he's dead."

The boy looked at Jack's newly shined boots, only a light coating of dust on the leather. "He's got a fine pair of boots, Pa."

"Leave 'em. He'll be dead soon, then you can take whatever you want. Get your rope, and let's get started." Elijah Rush looked at the two men whose ropes held Jack. "You boys get your ropes

---

back as soon as we have him snubbed up to that tree. Let's get it done."

There was no opening for Jack to make a move. The kid snatched his gun belt, and the two cowhands kept him cinched tight as they walked him under the tree limb. Vern threw the belt over his saddle, shook out a loop in his rope, and slapped it around Jack's neck. He yanked it tight before tossing the other end across the heavy limb of the barren old tree. The boy then grabbed the loose end and swung into his saddle.

Jack had faced imminent death before. He knew it wasn't over until he was dead. There was always a possibility of another chance, but it looked like those chances were dwindling fast. The boy pulled his rope tight, causing Jack to stand tall. He found, if he remained still and didn't try to suck air in too fast, he could still breathe.

"Alright, boys," Elijah Rush said to the two men with the ropes, "you can loose those ropes and pull 'em in."

Jack knew he had no opportunity unless he could get his hand on a gun. The only way to do that was from one of the men. If he could tangle a rope around his foot, he might be able to sucker the cowhand in close enough to grab him. It was at least worth a try. When the ropes fell, he jerked his feet, like he was trying to get the rope off, and managed to get one of the loops hung around his right foot and under his left heel.

"Dang it, Mr. Rush," he heard one of the men say. "Looks like my rope is hung. The feller is standing on it."

"Yeah, I see. I'm thinkin' we can fix that. Vern, why don't you back that horse of yours up a little. Lift that big feller off the ground a few inches. Let's give him a little taste of what's in store for him."

"Sure, Pa. Watch me."

Jack felt his hope fade when the loop tightened around his neck. He took a quick breath before his air was completely shut off. It felt like his throat was being pulled apart between the rope and the weight of his body. His eyes opened wide, and he began to rotate on the rope's end. His hands clutched at the noose. Unfortunately for Jack, no space remained for him to thrust his fingers between the hemp and his neck.

But the cowhand had gotten too close. With his remaining strength, for Jack could feel himself blacking out, he managed to kick the man square in the nose. He had the satisfaction of watching the blood spurt. But the feeling was short lived. The man wound up and drove his gloved fist straight into Jack's groin. If he hadn't been stretched, hanging from a rope, choking to death, he would have doubled over, the pain was so intense. It lasted only a few seconds, then everything faded.

When he awoke, he was curled on the ground, excruciating pain coming from his groin and his throat. *My throat,* he thought, and immediately grabbed for the rope.

Vern cackled in glee and backed his horse, pulling the rope tight again. Jack's body was yanked off the ground, and he kicked and turned on the rope, feeling himself sliding back down through the long dark tunnel to unconsciousness. Before his mind shut down, he thought he heard or felt a soft pop or crack. Had his neck broken? Was this the end?

Jack awoke again, and again he was curled up on the ground. The pain in his groin was bad, not as intense as it had been, but his throat was a living fire. His first thought was air, and he gasped, sucking it down.

Laughter pushed past his pain and made it to his mind. He willed strength into his arms and legs. He pushed himself to his knees and then to his hands. He didn't try to grab the rope. He needed time to get air to his lungs and body. When he was up, Jack could make out the grinning, laughing face of Elijah Rush floating in a red haze. He knew blood vessels were broken in his eyes. He had seen other men hanged, and they always had the broken vessels.

Rush stopped laughing but kept his grin. "You ain't near as

high and mighty as you were with yore guns, are you, Sage?" The outlaw leader let out a long laugh. "Look, boys, I swear he's lookin' taller. We must've stretched him at least an inch or two."

The other men laughed dutifully while Vern roared.

Jack glared at Rush. His voice was hoarse, just above a whisper. "Climb down from that horse, Rush. We can find out who's high and mighty."

Elijah Rush broke out in laughter again. "Look at him, men. He's still feisty. I'm half tempted to accommodate him."

Boone, his mouth wide in a snaggletoothed grin, looked at his pa. "Maybe you should, Pa. Teach that big bad marshal a thing or two."

Vern added his two cents. "Yeah, Pa. Whip him. We can hang him when you're done."

While their conversation continued, Jack scanned the other men. He wanted to remember each one. When he survived this hanging, he was going to find these men and bring them to justice, either the law's justice or his.

The cowhand next to Boone had graying hair and a thick handlebar mustache, well on its way to completely gray. His skin looked tough like well-tanned leather, a fella who had spent many years on the range. The face was not reflecting pleasure in what he was seeing, more resignation than anything else. Unlike the man next to him, who had a big grin and shiny bright blue eyes. Stringy blond hair hung to his shoulders, and he licked his lips in anticipation. *Maybe twenty-eight or nine,* Jack thought. He was one of the men who roped him.

On the other side next to Vern was the other roper. His gun hung low on his right side, and Jack could see the fancy tooling on the holster. The black-haired young man wore a brushed, black Stetson and black and gray striped pants. He showed no emotion, but watched through hard blue eyes with interest.

I'll not forget, Jack promised himself and switched his gaze back to Elijah Rush, who was talking.

The man shook his head. "No, boys. That's what he wants, and this feller ain't gittin' nothin' that he wants today." He stared down at Jack. "Look around, big man. See those green pines standin' tall? Feel that cold wind whipping you? You're seeing and feeling your last except for a mighty anxious rope. We're about to send you straight to Hell." He nodded to his youngest son. "Hang him, boy. Hang him high, I say."

7

Instead of waiting for the boy to yank the rope tight again, Jack leaped into the air, grabbing the noose and managing to press the fingers of both hands between the rope and his raw neck. The boy's response was not far behind his, backing his horse up quickly. Jack felt the noose jerk tight on his fingers, and the tiny space between the rope and his neck shrank to almost nothing but still allowed for a few short quick breaths. At the same time, he started swinging and jerking as hard as he could.

Rush and his men roared at the sight. They believed Jack was no longer breathing but kicking out in the final flailing of his death throes. He felt the arc lengthening and saw the edge of the cliff go by beneath him. The limb gave a soft but audible crack.

Jack's swing took him away from the edge. He paused momentarily and started back. Giving one final surge, knowing it would be his last, for even with his hands in the rope, his weight was pulling the noose tight about his neck, he put the last of his energy into the thrust.

There was a loud crack, almost like a rifle firing, and Jack was falling. He knew the rope would only be slack for a second or two before being jerked taut on Vern's saddle horn. With both hands and with every ounce of his remaining strength, Jack yanked the loop from both sides of his neck. It pulled wide, and he thrust it above his head just as it jerked tight again.

I'm free, his mind screamed. The thought flashed just before he struck the first rock, landing on his right shoulder. Pain seared through his already ravaged body. He bounced from the rock, flailing like a hay-stuffed scarecrow, and continued down the cliff. His body slammed into a large mahogany bush. Both hands grasped desperately for its tangled limbs, gripping, holding, slowing, and he crashed against the rocky slope. He could hear the distant yells of anger, and bullets peppered around him, ricocheting into the canyon.

Jack was no longer falling, but rolling, tumbling. A hip, then a shoulder, a thigh, every part of his body was taking a brutal beating from round and jagged rocks, some bruising, some gashing. Bullets slammed into the ground around him while his body bounced down the now sloping cliff side.

He crashed against another boulder and stopped. The crazy falling, rolling, and bouncing had ended. He lay there dazed but only for a moment. His mind was screaming, *Move, move, get away from the bullets. They keep coming.*

Through swollen, bloodshot eyes, he managed to see he was on a ledge. Just in front of him was a hollow.

He felt the hot burning slice of a bullet across the back of his lower left leg. Propelling himself forward with the last bit of his strength, he reached cover, safe from the searching bullets. It was not so much a cave, but what looked like a washed-out riverbank from a time long past. A time when the water wasn't so far beneath him, in the canyon, as it was now. Even as he scurried under the cover of the ledge, bullets continued to fly around the outside, pinging and glancing into the canyon. He dropped to the floor of his sanctuary, bloody and exhausted. Relief flowed over him.

He slept.

When he awoke, his left hand moved to his neck, which burned like someone had encircled it with a firebrand. His groin ached, but he knew, from having been hit there before, it would heal. He'd be fine, at least from that particular injury. The rest of his body felt as if every inch had been beaten with a jagged club. He carefully stroked his neck. The skin was raw and torn. The rope had done tremendous damage, but it should heal. There would be a huge, livid scar. With grim humor, he thought, *A scar is better than dead.*

Next, he tried to move his right arm. The sharp, tearing pain stopped him. *Out of joint,* he thought. He attempted to open his eyes, but they felt glued shut. No matter how much force he exerted, they wouldn't open. His good hand felt his left eye. It was the size of an orange. His fingers gently played across the right. It was bigger. They both felt like they were crusted over with blood and mud.

Jack began gently cleaning the crusty substance away. He spit on his fingers and used the saliva to soften the dried blood, gently working it from his eyelid. He had to take it slowly. He had no energy. Just lifting his good arm and expending the effort to clean his eye had almost exhausted him.

He lay quietly in his shelter. He couldn't see. He had no idea how badly he was hurt. He was stuck on the side of a canyon in the middle of nowhere. Panic began to creep into his mind, but he fought back. He had too often seen what it did to a man's reason. Once panic took over, the ability for rational thinking was gone. He didn't fight in that noose to live, only to throw it all away now that he was free. Jack began a deep breath. Halfway through it, another searing pain shot through his right side. A broken rib, at least one.

He exhaled and lay still. After a moment he began breathing as deeply as the broken rib would allow. He felt panic slithering away and sanity returning. He went back to cleaning his left eye.

He had no idea how long it took, but a crack of light finally glimmered beneath his partially raised eyelid. Everything was blurry, but at least he was seeing something. He continued to work on the eye. It opened wider, and he was able to see the outline of his sanctuary's entrance, the open space beyond, and the opposite canyon wall. He lay still, listening. There were no shots, no voices.

Jubilant with his success and the return of his vision, he switched to his more swollen right eye. This eye was swollen so badly, the lid, puffy and painful, refused to lift past a tiny crack, allowing some light but no definition. Unlike his left, which was clearing rapidly, the vision from his right eye was almost nonexistent. *It'll have to do for now,* he thought, and crawled to the edge of his cave.

Jack turned his head and looked down into the canyon with his good left eye. Though the fall had seemed to last forever, he was less than halfway to the river below. It looked like there was a narrow trail alongside the river. He needed to get down there. He needed water. It was daylight, still cloudy, but the wind had died. He couldn't see the sun, so he couldn't tell what time of day it was.

Time. His watch. Jack felt his heart leap at the thought of losing his watch, his last physical tie to his dead wife, Yasmina. He jerked his right hand to his inside vest pocket where he kept the watch, and felt the excruciating pain in his shoulder. Halting, he reached across with his left hand. Relief washed over him.

His watch was still there, safe in his pocket. He gave a quick prayer of thanks and removed the watch to examine it. His thumb caressed the emerald set in the cover, cut in the shape of the symbol of the French Foreign Legion, an exploding grenade. It remained secure. He flipped the watch open. Nine in the morning. It had been afternoon when Rush and his cronies found him. He must have slept through the night.

For the first time, he felt the cold attacking his body. He was shaking. He wiggled his toes—no feeling. Jack couldn't remove his boots for fear of his feet swelling and being unable to get them back on, but he had to do something. *If my feet freeze, I'll never get out of here,* he thought. He crawled back near one wall and lay on his back. Placing both feet on the wall, he began applying pressure. He pressed and released, pressed and released.

Jack continued his exercise. Time crawled by. His feet began to burn, but he kept it up. A side benefit was the exercise was warming his body. Finally, the burning subsided, and his feet felt as close to normal as he could expect. He crawled back to the edge of his cave. The pain in his shoulder was intense. He ran his left hand over the injured area. Sure enough, he could feel the lump where his shoulder had pushed back and out of the socket.

He lay on the cold ground, out of breath and spent. Lying near the edge, he could see down the slope. He examined the challenging, steep scree-covered slope. Jack knew getting down would be an impossible feat without first getting his shoulder back into place. He lay resting and planning his attempted route. The cold soaked through his bloody and ravaged body, sucking away his strength. Knowing he'd never have the strength to accomplish what lay ahead if he didn't get started this instant, he pushed himself erect with his left hand and began moving back.

On the back side of the cave, a rock jutted out from the smooth surface. With his back against the rock, the opposite wall was so close he couldn't stretch his legs, which was exactly what he needed. He scooted to the rock and pressed his back toward it. Using his left hand, he turned slightly, reached over his right shoulder, and felt the rock, its location, and his dislocated shoulder. Determined, he nodded. It was an almost perfect height. He slid his shoulder against it, bringing exquisite pain. Jack braced his feet against the opposite wall. As cold as it was, sweat glistened on his forehead. At the last second before he pushed, he remembered his broken rib and hoped he didn't puncture anything.

With all the force his devastated body could muster, he drove both of his long legs hard against the opposite wall. The shoulder resisted against the force, fighting the pain that emanated from the torn and damaged nerves. It held on the lip of the socket a moment, and slipped back in. When, at first, the shoulder had refused to slide into place, the pain was so great Jack almost quit, but the laughing face of Elijah Rush appeared to him. He summoned the last needed amount of strength, popped it into place, and collapsed.

Hours later, he regained consciousness. Jack opened his left eye, the right one still refusing to fully cooperate, and felt a little warmth. There was a bit of sunshine on the lip of his sanctuary. He rose and butt-scooted to the edge. The canyon was bathed in sunlight. He looked up to a clear sky.

The wind had moved on, and with it had gone the clouds. There was barely a breeze against the canyon wall. Jack eased to one edge of the small cave, looked up, and listened. He saw nothing, which with his eyes the way they were was no big accomplishment, but he also heard nothing. Nothing but the birds singing. That was a welcome sign.

Jack let his legs hang over the ledge and, with his left hand, felt his shoulder. From the outside it felt normal, but it was sore as the blazes. He raised both elbows and tried rotating them. Both worked. If he had to, he could use his right shoulder, but if he was smart, he would let it rest as much as possible. His stomach growled, reminding him that he hadn't eaten or drank anything since yesterday before noon. His mouth was dry, and making it even worse was the sound and sight of the river below him. Water was no more than four hundred yards away.

A thought struck him. The cookies. Both hands shot to his pockets. His right shoulder immediately warned him against making any quick movements. He found two cookies in his left coat pocket, along with a strip of jerky. He held his treasure in his big left hand. Making up his mind, he shoved one cookie and the jerky back into his pocket and broke a piece off the remaining cookie. *Thank you, Truman Shelby,* he thought.

Truman Shelby was a rancher near Denton, Texas. He raised quality horses along with cattle. They had met when Jack drove a herd to Missouri. He had needed a horse after recovering from being shot and left for dead. The bushwhacker had stolen his horse, Smokey.

Truman had been recommended to him, and Jack ended up buying not one, but three horses from the man. Jack observed Truman also fed his horses treats he called cookies. He gave Jack a sack of them plus the recipe. That had been a while back, but he still had the horses and the recipe. His horses and mule loved those cookies, and he had also developed a fondness for them. They were a mixture of molasses, carrots, oatmeal and apples, all mixed together, shaped into large cookies, and baked. Thank goodness he had a couple of them with him now.

He chewed slowly on the mixture. *I could sure use a hot cup of coffee to go with this, though I'd settle for water,* he thought. *They're a mite dry without a drink.* He swallowed the mouthful and took another bite, chewing while he looked over his task ahead and below. Scree, loose gravel, covered the remaining portion of the slope. It was interspersed with larger rocks and boulders. Scattered mahogany bushes were along the upper part of the slope. Lower, nearing the trail, the dark green mahogany grew thicker. It was going to be a rough trip down to the river.

For the first time, he felt good enough to examine his bullet wound. He already knew there was no broken bone. He just hoped it didn't tear up his calf muscle. It was sore but only now beginning to compete with his other pains. He pulled his pants leg up and laid his right leg across his left thigh. There it was, just below his knee and above the top of his tall boots. He was a lucky man. The bullet had burned a streak across his leg, leaving a lengthy cauterized channel, but at its deepest point, it couldn't be more than an eighth of an inch. *It hardly qualifies to be called a bullet wound,* he thought.

Jack pulled his pants leg down and checked the sun's position. Day was disappearing fast. He had to make up his mind, spend another night up here, or try to slide down the scree and get to water? He examined the river once more. Glistening in the afternoon sun, it was inviting but far away.

Movement.

He jerked back from the edge, sliding as deep into his little cave as he could go. Minutes slowly ticked by. Like a wounded bear, cautious but needing to know, he eased from inside the protection of his cave and moved his head slowly past the edge. His good eye peered down the slope and examined the brush along the river.

Deer. It was a small herd of mule deer, all bucks. Frightened by deer. He shook his head, feeling relieved and foolish at the same time. The animals were browsing on the mahogany bushes. Watching the deer, Jack took the time to examine the trail closer. What he had thought was a horse or human trail was actually a deer trail, used only by wild animals. It was too narrow to even have accommodated wild horses. He needn't be too concerned about humans, in the form of Rush and his gang or Apaches hunting along the narrow river. This, for all he knew, was a lost canyon. *There must be something blocking one end,* Jack thought, *or maybe both.*

And with the thought, he made up his mind. He needed water, and the only water was at the bottom of the canyon. There was a sage bush a third of the way down the slope. If he could hit that sage and slow his slide, he could keep his speed reduced. The lower his speed, the less chance of any more damage being done to his body. As bad as he already hurt, at least nothing but a rib was broken. The only other concerns were hitting another boulder, flipping over and rolling down the slope, or crashing into one of the tall scattered pines along the bottom.

Without considering it further, he pushed off the ledge and dropped onto the scree. He felt the gravel scraping and biting at his britches, but the sagebrush bush stopped him. His hands clutched at the thick branches, and he held tight.

Jack lay on the slope, close against the sage. His broken rib prevented deep breaths and hurt like the dickens from the slide, but the soft pungent odor of the sage helped relax him. His body stretched at an angle across the bush, resting and preparing for the longer slide. Feeling better than he thought he had a right to, he realigned his body down the slope and turned loose.

On the steep slope, he immediately began sliding. Accelerating rapidly, he whooshed by a large boulder, just missed a prickly pear, and slid for what seemed forever, gravel flying. At last, the slope began to level, and the mahogany thicket rushed toward him.

He had no directional control, but at least he wasn't tumbling. He slammed into the brush, limbs tearing at his skin and clothing. Brought to an almost instant stop, Jack sat, stunned.

He was no longer on the steep incline, but almost level. Water leaped over the rocks less than twenty feet in front of him. He grasped a handful of brush and tried to stand. His weakness surprised him. It took a second attempt before he was able to drag his torn and bloody body erect. He could feel his leg muscles quivering. He pushed around the bush he had slammed into, turned sideways to pass between two others, and stood in the open. The water was directly to his front, only a few feet away. His throat was beyond parched, but before stepping forward for his much-needed drink, he looked around.

Thirty yards down the river stood the mule deer. Three of them, heads down, continued to feed while the remaining two chewed and watched him. They were calm, completely disinterested in his arrival. It was obvious the muleys were not familiar with humans and the dangers they brought. Their antlers were fully developed and covered in velvet. Most of the velvet had been torn loose. A little remained, hanging in strips. Their rubbing would soon clean them to sharp points. One buck, his head down pulling at the leaves, displayed a huge set of antlers. He yanked his head, tearing a mouthful of leaves from the bush, raised it high, and chewed, studying the intruder.

Jack's thirst overrode his interest in deer. He examined the canyon up the river, to the east. It was silent and still. Satisfied, he shuffled to the water, a mass of aching bones and flesh, and slowly knelt. He removed his leather gloves from his hands and worked his fingers. His hands had survived much better than the rest of his body. The gloves had saved him. Though the leather was cut and torn, they were still basically intact. They would continue providing warmth and protection. Using his cupped left hand, he scooped and drank, scooped and drank. The water was cold and sweet as it played across his tongue, caressing his aching throat. It felt as good as it tasted.

He scooped a handful and washed his face, all the while, his head moved, checking both directions. The deer continued to browse. He scrubbed at both eyes, cleaning them and cooling his scratched and fevered cheeks and forehead. In the eddy where he was drinking, he could see his reflection. Amazed at the battered face staring back at him, he did not recognize himself. It was twice its normal size and covered with cuts and punctures. His eyes were huge from the swelling, like two round, puffy red orbs. There was a gash across his forehead that, after being washed, oozed a thin bloody liquid.

He pushed himself erect.

Except for natural sounds, birds, the mule deer chewing, an owl hooting down the canyon, there was nothing else. No humans, white or brown. It was like he was alone in Eden. Thoughts ran through Jack's mind. *After what I've endured, this is certainly no Eden, but it could be if it weren't for Rush and his bunch.*

Even so, I'm mighty thankful for surviving. I've been in some tight spots, even shot and left for dead, but I don't think I've ever been in one like this. If that limb hadn't broken when it did, I'd be hanging there stretching Vern's rope.

Lord, I'm not much on praying, but let me say thanks. If you hadn't been with me yesterday and today, I'd be talking to you face-to-face. I'm much obliged. Now, if you could stick with me a while longer.

8

Jack looked back up the canyon wall where he had fallen. He could see several of the limbs of the old tree jutting out over the edge. He examined his route of travel from the tree to where he stood, and shook his head. It was impossible that he was here, standing at the bottom of this canyon, alive. It was a sheer wall, changing to a slope just before where his cave was located. Huge rocks and boulders lay in the path he had traveled. As he stared, he saw the small bush that caught him in front of his cave, and the shallow indentation in the side of the rocks. It looked so small from here. He shook his head in disbelief of what he had been through over the past few days. Thirst called again, and he turned back to the river.

He drank several more handfuls of the crystal-clear water and washed his face and eyes again. He bent closer to the water as he rubbed his face. Through the ripples, he caught a glint among the broken rocks on the bottom of the clear stream. Jack tilted his head slightly more to the left. His eye seemed to focus better in that position. He moved his face closer to the water's surface. The glint was still there. It hadn't moved. It definitely wasn't a fish. He yanked his coat off and laid it to the side. After making sure his gloves were still in the coat pocket, and pushing his shirt and long johns sleeve up to his shoulder, Jack thrust his hand into the water. The cold bit at his cuts and scratches. Jack felt around the gravel and clutched a small, smooth rock. Lifting it from the water, he thought, *That's a heavy sucker.* He pulled it clear and held it in the sunlight, turning it over again and again.

With each turn he became more excited. It was exactly as Hank had described, a nugget. A big gold nugget. He hefted it. This was no fool's gold. It was the real thing. *At least four or five ounces,* he thought, *maybe more.* The next thought brought a sardonic grin to his face, even though it hurt. *Thanks, Rush. You may have just made me a rich man.*

His grin widened as he examined the nugget. It was solid gold. He shoved his thumbnail into the soft metal. It left a deep gouge. Dropping the nugget into his coat pocket, he knelt back at the riverbank, turned his head again, and searched the water. Another glint. Was it possible? He reached in and pulled out a twin to the first nugget.

Jack couldn't believe it. He pulled the other nugget from his vest pocket and, using the thumb and forefinger of each hand, held them side by side. They were twins. He shook his head. The deer continued to browse nearby, and the owl hooted again. Jack turned to the deer and held out the two nuggets. "How lucky can a man get?"

The mule deers' heads jerked up at his voice. Big brown eyes stared at him for a few seconds, but determining they were still safe, heads dropped, and they went back to eating. Jack returned to the stream's edge and peered into the water. There were golden glints all over the bottom. They were everywhere. The shiny gold flashes extended out into the current until the depth and white water obscured them from sight.

Feeling the air growing cooler, he rolled his sleeve down, picked up his coat, and slipped it on. He took as deep a breath as his ribs would allow, turned, and started slowly walking upstream, searching for more of the gold. The sun drifted lower in the west, but Jack continued walking and looking. He was entranced by the golden flashes he continued to see on the bottom. He came to a steep-banked dry wash emptying into the river. He stopped and looked around.

Surprised, Jack saw how far he had come up the river. Looking back, he realized it had been like a trance. The gold had caused a spell of sorts to come over him. He had heard of men with gold fever. Many had died from the madness in their quest for the precious metal. "Get a grip on yourself," Jack said to himself. "This gold won't do you a blamed bit of good if you die out here."

For the first time, he realized it had grown darker. The only remaining light was above the rim. He needed a fire and food. He felt his legs growing weaker. He looked up at the canyon rim. In his fever, he had forgotten all about Rush and his men. They could have ridden along the rim looking for him. Wandering along the bottom of the canyon, he would have been easy to spot. With relief, he realized if they had spotted him, they would have started shooting. He thought about them warm at their ranch, and he could feel an anger building deep inside.

But he also felt something else. Dizziness. Maybe not dizzy, more light-headed. He needed a fire. However, he needed a place for it so it couldn't be seen from the canyon's edge. Though he didn't think it true, because none of Rush's gang had shown up along the river, there might be access to this canyon Rush knew about. Jack couldn't take the chance of making his location and the fact he was alive known. He looked over the edge of the draw. The bottom, in the fading light, was faint at best. The edge was too high for him to jump, especially being so weak, plus the broken rib. He turned and started walking up the draw. The slope gradually steepened. He started to turn around when the draw made a sharp turn to the right, turning east, and deepened further.

Jack followed the circular edge, dodging several mahogany and sagebrush bushes. Between several, hidden from sight until a person crossed it, he found a trail he could barely see in the dim light. The trail had been in use so long, it was cut deep, maybe a foot, into the side of the draw. Where it entered the draw, it turned and angled across the sloping side. After taking three steps down into the trail, he was able to hold onto the upper edge until he reached the bottom of the draw. Dark had fallen, and it wouldn't be long before it would be pitch black. He wouldn't be able to see his hand in front of his face. The cold was cutting through his battered coat and torn britches.

He found a few broken, dried twigs. It was enough to get a fire started. He moved them to the base of the draw's bank on the side of the canyon wall. The wash, or draw, or cut, was over six feet deep, which would prevent anyone from seeing a small fire from the north canyon wall. Jack reached for his lucifers. He always kept four of them in his pocket, knowing he could get caught away from his horse and saddlebags, or his mule, Stonewall.

He fumbled in the dark with his right hand. There was no pocket. The pocket and the contents were missing. All that remained was fabric flapping in the breeze. The side pocket had been completely ripped out. He jerked his left hand into the coat's opposite pocket and breathed a sigh of relief. The Barlow knife his father had given him was still there. He normally kept it on his right side, but for some reason he had put it in the left pocket. If he had followed his routine, the knife would have been gone along with the matches and his packet of caps for his pistols. Jack felt a flood of relief. His Barlow wasn't a knife he'd use in self-defense. It was a gift from his father, who had told him, "It will help with chores your whole life." It had survived his shipwreck, his fighting in Algiers, the war, his trek through Mexico, and the cattle drive to Missouri. He began a sigh, but the pain from his broken rib stopped him.

Jack shoved the knife back into his pocket, ensured it was

secure and, with a large flat rock he had found, felt his way to the base of the bank. Using the rock, he began digging the soft sand in an attempt to make a more comfortable and hopefully warmer bed. Reaching the depth and length he wanted, he crawled in, backing against the wall. Lying in the dirt, his head cradled on a big hand, he thought about the time he had wasted searching for gold. *I could have cut a few boughs from the younger pines and gathered needles. At least those would have provided a little insulation and padding. Now, I'm lying here in this cold dirt.* He berated himself a while longer, then started planning his actions after he returned to Silver City. It was going to be a grim day for the Rush family.

Finally, even through the pain and cold, he closed his eyes and fell asleep. Jack's sleep was fitful. Dreams, of happiness and battles, of love and death, filled his restless hours. He would wake, lie in his frigid sand bed shaking, and drift back to sleep. The hours passed, and as they slipped by, his restlessness increased.

He jerked awake as the sky was beginning to lighten in the east. His eye opened, and he lay in his bed, gazing out at four eyes staring at him.

He lay motionless.

Two coyotes sat on their haunches no more than ten feet from Jack. Their tongues lolled from their mouths and alternately curled and extended as they breathed.

"What do you boys want?" Jack asked.

They both jumped to their feet, eyes fixed on Jack. He worked himself out of his bed and turned so he was facing them, his back against the bank and his arms wrapped around his drawn-up legs, and introduced himself. "Morning, I'm Jack Sage."

One of the coyotes had begun pacing back and forth. He stopped, his head canted slightly to the left.

"If you boys would go catch me a rabbit, I'd be much obliged." Jack watched the two of them for a few more minutes. "Alright, it's time I got started since it looks like you two aren't going to be any help." He pushed himself to his feet.

The coyotes watched until he was half-erect, then turned, trotted up the trail he had come down, and disappeared over the edge of the wash. Jack stretched and flexed his lower back, watching the two coyotes, in single file, trot along the trail. In the faint, early morning light, he turned, scanning the north canyon wall and the hanging tree. The tree looked small from here. As he gazed, his hand subconsciously traveled to his neck. Just touching the exposed flesh jolted him. *I've got to get this cleaned again,* he thought.

His hand started for the horizontal gash across his forehead and froze. Two horsemen had appeared by the tree. Jack dropped to the floor of the wash and hugged the side. *If they haven't already seen me, they won't see me now. I've got to clean these cuts and get a drink. If I stay below the edge of the wash, they won't be able to see me until they get into a position where they're able to look down the length of it.*

He stretched back up to the edge of the wash and peered over the top. The riders were along the canyon's rim, moving in his direction. He turned and looked at the inviting water and dropped back down. *I'll have to wait until they're gone. I can't take a chance on being seen.* Though his thirst was strong, he relaxed against the bank of the wash.

He was sitting next to the bed he had dug out. There had been a rock poking in his back. He bent and scraped some of the dirt aside. A bright gleam greeted him. He wiped more away. Another nugget, and the sand was covered with tiny flecks of gold. His hand worked quickly, dislodging the stone. It was huge. It was at least twice the size of the other two he had found. It was more jagged, but still soft. His thumbnail pressed an indentation in the surface.

Jack shook his head and did a bit of rapid math. *At twenty bucks an ounce, and guesstimating sixteen ounces, I've got three*

hundred and twenty dollars' worth of gold in these three little nuggets.
He looked in his old bed at the tiny gold flakes covering the
disturbed sand and dirt. A soft chuckle escaped him. *That may
have been a golden bed last night, but it was a danged uncomfortable
one. Although, if I can get out of here alive and get back into this
canyon, it just might qualify as a bonanza.* He felt like leaping with
joy and excitement, but restrained himself. That was all he
needed to do with those riders on the canyon's edge, but as soon
as they were gone, he would clean himself up and try to find a
way out of this canyon.

Jack waited an hour after the riders disappeared before he
eased to the mouth of the wash. The first thing he did was calm
his thirst. Then, while keeping an eye on the rim, he stripped out
of his torn clothing and slipped into the water. It was cold, feeling
both welcome and painful in his cuts and scrapes. His right
shoulder ached, but he could move it. Several bruises were sore
to the touch, now turning blue and green, hopefully a sign of
healing. Finished, he stepped from the water, feeling better than
he had any right to expect.

I can't believe I made it through this without anything broken, he
thought as he pulled on his torn britches. He finished dressing
while continuing to scan both rims of the canyon, Remembering
the cookie and piece of jerky, he yanked them from his pocket.

Jack bit off a piece of the cookie and chewed. The combina-
tion of apple, molasses, carrots, and oatmeal was like ambrosia.
He tried to slow his eating as much as possible, but in moments
he was chewing the last bite. He swallowed and looked at the
jerky. With his mouth watering, he shoved it back into his pocket.
It would have to wait until later.

He gazed at the wash where it disappeared into the trees
higher up the canyon wall. He would follow it. It might show him
a way out of this canyon, but first he wanted to see how far up the
river the gold was visible. He climbed up the opposite side of the
draw, took a few steps, and saw nothing. There were no flashes,

no golden nuggets, nothing glimmered in the water. They ended at the mouth of the wash. He turned, and his eyes followed the wash up the canyon wall. *So you hold the secret of the gold. You might also show me the way out of here, but first I'm checking the river. It might hold the secret exit.* He faced forward and continued along the riverbank.

Jack hadn't traveled far before he heard the roar of white water ahead. Rounding a bend in the river, he was confronted with a mass of boulders and rapids. The bank was no longer passable, blocked by huge boulders and the narrowing canyon. He stared at the maelstrom crashing through the canyon. *There's no way a human could survive that, but there's still the wash,* Jack thought. He turned and retraced his steps.

The exertion was taking a toll on his bruised, beaten, and starved body. He moved to a tall pine, kicked a couple of cones out of the way, and sat, using the tree for a backrest. It was a smaller pine, no more than a foot in diameter, and fit his back perfectly. The pain in his injured shoulder subsided, but he felt flushed, feverish. He couldn't worry about it now. He had to get out of this canyon.

Jack gazed along the path he had traveled. This was beautiful virgin country. It was possible he might not only be the first white man in this canyon, but the first man. He enjoyed the feeling. Jack had always known, since he was a youngster, he was a loner. He worked better by himself. He enjoyed the quiet, his time alone. Not to say he didn't like people, but, except for the friends he had made, and his short marriage to Yasmina, the only woman for him, he was at his best alone. This canyon atmosphere was perfect for him.

He gave a soft, deriding chuckle. *Almost perfect. Perfect would be armed, with food, a horse, and a way out of here.* With that thought, and as rested as he was going to get, Jack pushed himself erect. For a moment he felt faint, but he steadied himself and continued back to the draw. He walked through the scattered pines, the morning sun warming the canyon bottom and him. The warmth penetrated his injured body, relaxing the strained and bruised muscles.

Throughout his morning trek, he had constantly examined the shallow water along the bank. There had been no further sign of gold. Reaching the wash, still standing on the high bank, he could see tiny pieces of gold glinting in the sand and among the rocks where the dry wash joined the river. He found the spot he had climbed out, hung onto the edge, and dropped to the bottom.

Prior to beginning his trek up the dry wash, he stepped over to the mouth where it joined the river. Flecks of gold glinted in the sand all around him. The fever rumbled beneath the surface of his mind, driving him to search for nuggets on the land and in the water, but common sense won. He had to get out of here, and he had solved his two questions. One, whether there was an outlet up the river, and two, did the gold come from the wash?

Jack knelt and drank until he thought he might explode. He had no idea how long it would be before he would taste water again. Rising, he gave one last look at the bonanza he had found, turned, and began wading through the sand. Not far past where he had slept the night before, the wash meandered to the right, parallel to the rim, and entered a thick stand of pines. Once in the trees, Jack was no longer concerned with being discovered by anyone on the canyon rim.

9

J ack continued his hike along the bottom of the wash. Tufted-eared squirrels fussed at him from the pine tops, a porcupine shuffled through the pine needles, ignoring his passage, and a mockingbird sang an interminable song. His normally strong legs grew weary as the wash climbed through the trees.

The slope steepened abruptly, and jutting from the wall of the wash were jagged sections of what Jack thought mimicked Hank's description of rotten quartz. He stopped and, while holding an exposed pine root to maintain his balance on the slanting bottom, grasped a portion of a thinner piece of the brittle quartz. It easily broke off in his hand. Thick gold streaks ran through the soft quartz. Jack stared at the rock. Was it possible? Half joking, he had told Hank he was lucky. He had been lucky with the herd of cattle driven from Texas to Missouri. They'd arrived with minimal loss, and the price of beef had been high.

His mind wandered back to Texas. He had pitched in with Montana Huff and Bronco Fenn, investing in a herd to take to Missouri. After their successful drive, they had returned to Texas and bought a ranch. He tossed most of his money in the pot for the purchase. Montana and Bronco wanted to make him a one-third partner, but he refused. Though he had put up a third of the money, he wouldn't be contributing any of the sweat or effort to build their ranch. If they were successful, he'd be reaping the benefits just like they would, so he told them he'd do the deal only if they gave him twenty percent instead of thirty-three. Montana and Bronco would split the remaining eighty percent. The two friends and partners agreed, and Jack owned a partnership in their Texas ranch. He hadn't heard from them in over a year. *Hope they're doing good,* he thought. *They deserve it. One of these days I'll wander—*

His head jerked up. Had he heard a yell? He waited, at last shaking his head. He shoved the piece of gold-laden quartz into his coat pocket, along with the nuggets, and started up the wash. He had taken only three steps when again he heard the faint call, followed by a shot, and then another. He compelled his sore, fevered body to climb faster.

The wash steepened and narrowed. Jack pushed hard. His breathing was labored, his muscles ached, but he thrust himself upward. Someone was in trouble and needed help. The wash had deepened to where Jack, even at his height, couldn't be seen from the sides. He was holding protruding rocks and boulders as handholds, pushing with his legs. The floor of the wash was only inches from his face, almost vertical. He was kicking holes in the dirt with his boots and grasping exposed roots and rocks to pull himself up.

Jack had to stop, but there was no place to rest. He could either climb up or slide down. If his foot stayed in a hole too long, the ground would begin to give way from his weight. His breath was coming in gasps and with such force, it was blowing dust out of the wash into his face, but he pressed on.

He looked down once between his body and the wash and decided not to repeat that mistake. Looking down the wash was almost like looking over the edge of the canyon where the hanging tree was located. It wasn't quite vertical, but enough so that if he began to fall, he wouldn't stop for at least a hundred feet. *I sure hope there's a way over the rim, or I am in deep trouble.* He kept gasping and climbing.

Suddenly the wash shallowed to the point it was almost level with the surrounding vertical terrain. As far as Jack could see to his left and right and above him were mahogany bushes. They were clinging as desperately as he was to the canyon wall. The problem was the wash was so shallow the bushes were also growing in it, providing obstacles. However, they also provided handholds.

The limbs pushed and scraped at his face and arms. His body was shaking from the exertion, and he was finding it difficult to grip with his big hands. His hands, like his legs and arms, were weakening. Collecting all the strength he could muster, his biceps bulging, he gave one more heave, pulling himself beyond the next bush.

He was looking over the edge of the rim past additional bushes, but they were sparse enough for him to see the pine forest. The top of the rim, at last. He held his position and scanned from left to right through the mahogany. He saw two saddled horses ground hitched, but he couldn't see the men.

Finding a solid rock to brace his left foot against, Jack shoved, at the same time pulling at the bushes he was clinching. His thick upper body heaved over the top, and he lay with legs sticking straight out above the canyon rim. But not for long. He belly crawled away from the edge, under the bushes, and collapsed. It felt as if every muscle in his body was quivering, even his insides were shaking, and he felt feverish.

His lungs demanded heavy fast breathing, but he willed himself to slow and breathe quietly. Minutes passed. He lay there, slowly recovering. The quivering ceased, and his breathing, though high, was not gasping. He listened and watched.

The mahogany bushes extended about ten feet beyond the

edge of the canyon. They gave way to open rocks for thirty feet to where the pines began. The horses were at the edge of the pines, cropping what little grass they could find in the rocks. Jack eased to the edge of the bushes and listened before making his move. Rifles rested in scabbards on both horses. If he could get to one, he'd be armed.

He heard laughing, and then a cowhand appeared, walking through the trees toward the horses. Jack's anger began to rise. He recognized the man as one of Rush's men. Jack had seen him at the saloon when they shot up the courthouse. The man was laughing. He reached his horse, pulled his canteen from his saddle, and took a long swig. Jack could hear someone call from deep in the forest, but couldn't understand what he said.

"Alright, I'm coming, but we'd better be getting back to the ranch, or the boss will skin us alive. You know he wants a report on Sage." The man laughed again. "As if anyone could survive a fall off that canyon wall." The cowhand hung his canteen back on the saddle and shouted to his unseen partner, "Course, he was probably dead from the hangin' afore he ever hit those rocks." He walked away, disappearing in the trees.

Jack made his move. There was no hesitation. He was up and running for the closest horse. He reached the animal, pulled the Winchester from its scabbard, and worked the lever just enough to ensure there was a round in the chamber. He eased the chamber closed and quietly pulled the hammer all the way back to full cock. After patting the horse on the neck, he swung into the saddle. *Goodness,* he thought, *it feels fine to be in a saddle again.* He began riding slowly in the direction of the cowhand.

Through the pines, he could hear them talking. "They gave us quite a chase. Guess they want me to earn my attention."

"Yeah, they're both mighty pretty for Injuns. Too bad that one broke her leg."

There was silence for a moment, then the first speaker said,

"You know, after we're done, we're gonna have to kill 'em. They tell anyone, them 'Paches will be looking for our scalps."

"What about the baby?"

"Leave it, kill it, don't make no difference. It'll die either way."

Jack's thoughts went to his dead baby son, killed by the assassin who had killed his wife. His face flushed with rage. Usually in a fight, he was cold, detached, but now he felt that same rage he had felt so long ago coming over him. He slapped his heels into the horse's flanks. The animal leaped forward, bursting into the clearing. The grins on the outlaws' faces froze at the appearance of this bloody and bruised demon from hell charging them.

The man with the gun was so stunned by Jack's appearance, he froze. The gun drooped toward the ground. Jack rode the horse directly at him. Before the cowhand could come out of his shock, the horse hit him with a shoulder, knocking him spinning.

The man who had gone for a drink managed to get his six-gun out of his holster. Jack turned in the saddle, handling the Winchester like a pistol. Though Jack's vision was still blurry, the muzzle came to bear on the cowhand, and he pulled the trigger. The Winchester roared, and the bullet slammed into the man's belly, driving him back against a tree. With the shock of the bullet and the tree, his six-gun flew across the forest floor.

Jack reined the horse around in time to see the man grab his belly with both hands and slide down the pine, stopping when he hit the ground. Whipping around, Jack's eyes found the other man. This was the one who had talked about killing the baby. He lay prone on his back, gripping his shoulder, his face contorted with pain.

Jack glanced at the two Indian women to ensure neither had been attacked. They returned his gaze. He pulled the horse to a stop, leaped from its back, and dropped the reins to the ground. Neither man was anxious to pick up a gun. The gutshot man lay moaning against the tree, and the one the horse had hit was flat on his back, holding his shoulder and staring at Jack like he was looking at a ghost.

The two Apache women, one holding a baby, remained calm. Dark, steady eyes watched him with suspicion. The one with the baby had both legs stretched in front of her, her left canted unnaturally toward the right. The skin bulged above the break.

He walked to the cowhand holding his shoulder, straddled him, and stuck the muzzle of the rifle against his forehead so hard blood began to flow. The man tried to move his head away from the pain.

"Don't move, or I'll blow your head off."

The man stopped, blood flowing down the side of his cheek, and grimaced with pain. "Don't shoot me. I didn't try to hang you."

Jack leaned over and turned his head slightly to the left so he could clearly see this worthless piece of dung. His throat was still sore from the rope, and he had not spoken since the hanging. His voice came out like a hoarse growl. "You think this was about a hanging? I heard you talking about killing those women and the baby. I should gutshoot you, too." He moved the muzzle of the Winchester down to the man's belly.

"No! No! No!" the man screamed, and started begging. "Please, Mr. Sage. Don't shoot me. I was just talking. We weren't gonna hurt them Injuns. I swear on my poor ma's grave."

Jack's rage turned to disgust. He swung the barrel of the Winchester and slapped the man in the side of the head. The cowhand collapsed. Jack unfastened the outlaw's gun belt, pulled it from under him, and fastened it around his waist. He took a step to where the man's gun had fallen, picked it up, checked the barrel and cylinder were clear, and dropped it into his holster. Next he strode over to the man he had gutshot.

The man looked up at him. "You look terrible, mister."

Jack nodded. "You try getting hanged and jumping off a cliff. See how great you look."

The man's voice was flat, emotionless. "You killed me. You know that?"

Jack nodded. "Aimed to. Sorry I hit low. My eyes are a little messed up from the fall." He picked up the man's gun and slid it behind his gun belt, turned, and walked over to the two women. Jack knew a little sign language, but no Apache. That was what he figured these women were. He squatted far enough away so they would not feel threatened, and made the sign of friend. They both watched him apprehensively and stared at him. The woman's leg needed to be straightened and splinted. He pointed to it and, with both hands, mimed pulling something apart.

The two women spoke to each other in a language he did not understand, looked back at him, and nodded. The uninjured woman pointed at him, moved her hand up and down in front of her, and made poking motions with her hands toward her body and face. Jack moved forward and dropped to his knees next to the woman with the broken leg. He turned, pointed to the edge of the cliff, and with his hands, simulated going over the cliff.

They showed the first emotion he had seen from them since he arrived. Their dark brown eyes grew large, and the uninjured woman began speaking rapidly to the one with the broken leg, who kept shaking her head. Jack made the motion of going over the cliff again and nodded emphatically. The younger woman, the uninjured one, pointed to Jack's neck. Jack pointed to the man who was still lying on the ground, out cold, then back at himself, tilted his head, and held his hand above his head like hanging from a noose. The younger woman's eyes narrowed. She glared at the man on the ground and spat.

Jack leaned over the older woman's broken leg, examining the injury. It was already beginning to turn blue. He looked into her dark eyes and nodded. Holding the baby close, she stared at Jack, took a deep breath, and dipped her head in acknowledgment.

Jack grasped her ankle in one of his big hands, the other held her knee, and he pulled, like pulling a knot tight. He felt bone scrape against bone. She gave a single gasp from the pain, and the broken bone slipped into place. He raised his head to look at the woman. Sweat had popped out on her forehead, and her eyes were closed tight. But other than the gasp, those were the only indications she was in pain.

She never screamed, he thought. He nodded to her and then mentally kicked himself. He had forgotten to have splints handy. Looking around, he saw a thick straight limb, about the right length, by the grazing horse. Jack held up a finger and rose to his feet. He walked over to the limb, picked it up, and jerked a couple of piggin' strings from the saddle. He strode back, snapped the limb in half, and placed one on each side of her leg. Pulling out his Barlow, Jack cut the leather piggin' string in half, tied the sticks above and below the break, leaned back, and viewed his handiwork. It wasn't the best in the world, but it would hold until they could get back to their camp. The two of them could ride the smaller horse. He'd take the larger, the one he had originally chosen.

He rose and headed for the man with the injured shoulder. The outlaw watched him with guarded eyes. Jack never said a word. He reached down, grabbed the man by the shoulder, and flipped him over. He was greeted with a shout of pain. The woman killer yelled again when his arms were pulled behind him, and Jack tied them at the elbows.

"Oh, man, you can't tie me up like this. It's killin' my shoulder."

Jack felt his rage boiling. It built into an almost uncontrollable urge to put a bullet right between the man's eyes. But he refrained. "You're a big baby. That woman didn't utter a sound when I set her leg. Shut up, or I'll send them over here to silence you permanently." The outlaw's mouth slammed shut, and his complaining ceased.

Jack left the clearing to retrieve the other horse. After a short walk through the forest, he could see the animal grazing at the treeline. It raised its head and chewed as Jack approached. Drawing near, he moved slowly and spoke softly to the animal, grasped the reins, rubbed its neck, and talked to it for a few minutes. He started to swing into the saddle, but changed his mind. The clearing wasn't far. He turned to lead the horse back to the group when a man's scream split the quiet forest. Swinging up the Winchester, he found himself surrounded by Apaches. Lances were thrust inches from his chest. He slowly lowered the rifle.

They appeared like ghosts from the trees. A wide-shouldered, slim-waisted man wearing only a loincloth sat on a dark brown sorrel. His Winchester rested with its butt plate on his thigh, the muzzle pointing skyward, and the man's right hand around the grip. He watched Jack with indiscernible eyes that were so brown they looked black.

The younger woman came running through the forest. She didn't stop until she reached the man with the rifle. Her right hand rested on his thigh and her left on the horse's shoulder. She spoke rapidly. Jack couldn't understand a word.

Great, Jack thought, *no good deed goes unpunished. I survive the hanging, climb out of that blasted canyon, and save the damsels, and what do I get for it? Scalped. Can my day get any better?*

The man affectionately touched the woman's hair, said something to her, turned to his men, and spoke again. They lowered their weapons.

The Indian looked him up and down, his eyes stopping at Jack's neck. There was a faint, almost indiscernible lift to the corners of his mouth. In English the man said, "My daughter says for me not to kill you. But from the looks of you, it is possible you will be in my debt if I do."

Great, Jack thought, *an Apache with a sense of humor. I might just die laughing.* Jack nodded his head. "I'm obliged, though it might put me out of my pain, I reckon I'd just as soon hang around a while longer."

The Indian returned the nod, his face unreadable. "I am chief of the Chiricahua Apache. My daughter tells me you saved them."

Jack shook his head. "Don't know that I did. You folks would have probably showed up in time. I just happened to climb out of that canyon at the right place. I heard a couple of yells and came to see."

The chief eyed Jack's weapons. "They are not scratched or dented. You must have taken them from these dogs."

"It wasn't hard. When I came out of the canyon, their horses were the first things I saw. They left them right there for me to take, rifles in the scabbards."

"Yet you did not think of yourself. You did not mount a horse and run, but rescued my daughter and wife. When you were finished with the white dogs, you repaired my wife's leg. You have been busy for a man with such a"—he hunted for an English word, couldn't find it, and said—"beaten body."

The exertion of the climb, his injuries and fever, and the flow of adrenaline had put more of a demand on Jack's body than he realized. He stood listening to the chief speak and marveled at how the man's horse began to float in the air, slowly drifting away. Somewhere in his fading conscious, he realized it wasn't the horse floating away, it was him.

His knees folded.

For a fleeting moment, before darkness set in, he heard the whish of moccasins in the pine needles and felt strong hands grasp and hold him.

10

J ack loved quail hunting, especially with his papa, Uncle
Teddy, and their two exuberant English pointer bird dogs,
Ginger and Spicy. Today was a special day. He had been
looking forward to this since reaching his tenth birthday
on January the twentieth of this year. It had been a long wait, but
the magic day was finally here. It was the day after Christmas,
and he was hunting with his brand-new single-barrel, twelve-
gauge shotgun. His hand caressed the smooth maple forearm
while his eyes tracked the dogs.

The two pointers were cutting through the short grass on the
Virginia hillside, heads to the ground, searching for the scent of
the little brown bombs, bobwhite quail. The smell of pine trees
filled Jack's young nose. He wanted to run with the dogs, but he
had his new single-barrel in hand, and Papa had taught him to be
careful with the weapon, and that included no running.

Passing a small but thick patch of grass, Spicy wheeled to a
sudden stop, her head down, nose pointed toward the patch. The
dog's white and liver-spotted body was twisted almost into the
shape of a U, frozen with tail extended and stiff. Her intelligent
eyes locked on the grass patch. The other pointer, Ginger, had

seen Spicy go into a point and dashed toward her until they were less than ten feet apart. She slowed and stalked the remaining distance. Each foot lifted, quivering in anticipation, slowly stepping toward Spicy until she was slightly behind and to her left and locked in the same rigor as her partner.

"Easy," Papa said, "easy, girls. Hold." The word hold was drawn out like it had three long *o*'s in it, in a commanding but gentle and persuasive tone. The two men and Jack slowly moved forward, Jack slightly in front of and between his uncle and papa, until they were within feet of the dogs.

Jack stared at the small patch of grass, trying to see the bobwhites, but he saw nothing. He looked up at his papa to speak his disbelief into existence, when the grass exploded.

Brown and white bombs blasted from the patch, wings whirring so fast they were only a blur. His shotgun snapped to his shoulder, right thumb cocking the hammer as the shotgun rose. The weapon settled into his shoulder like it was meant to be there. His eyes picked out one of the little missiles, forgetting the distracting vision and sound of the others. He could hear his papa's voice, "Choose a single target, son, don't try to hit them all." The muzzle caught up with the bird and slid well past. He had to lead the feathery little creature, or his shot string would end up behind it.

When it felt right, he pulled the trigger. A moment later, the shotgun roared, slamming his shoulder. He rocked back only slightly, because he was leaning into the shot, and through the smoke he could see his bird puff with the strike of the birdshot, cease flying, and begin to fall.

A fraction of a second later, Papa's and Uncle Teddy's shotguns roared and roared again, each firing twice. Feathers exploded from four additional quail, and their graceful flight ended with tumbling falls, plummeting to the earth. The two men and Jack watched the remaining birds halt their wing beats and sail through the timber, cutting back and forth around the trees until, as a covey, they piled into another stand of grass fifty yards ahead.

The dogs held their points until Jack's papa spoke. "Go fetch," and they were off and running. Ginger dashed to the nearest bird, picked it up, moved a few feet to her left, and while softly moving the dead quail already in her mouth, she picked up a second and, with tail whipping, raced straight back to Papa.

Uncle Teddy, watching the dogs, laughed and pointed at Ginger. "Look at that dog, she has two birds in her mouth." He shook his head. "What a dog." He looked down at Jack, a wide grin splitting his leathery sun-browned face. "Now this is the way to spend the day after Christmas."

Jack thought, *It sure is, Uncle Teddy. This is my first quail with my new shotgun.* He eyed his new single-shot proudly and turned his gaze to his tall papa. He was a strong man. He'd heard his ma talking to his aunt about how handsome his pa was. He wondered, *Is that what handsome is? He looks strong and kind to me.*

Before beginning the reload of his shotgun, his pa grinned down at Jack. "That was a good shot, son. Having fun with that new twelve?"

"Yes, sir, this is the best day of my life."

His papa, Ginger and Spicy, and Uncle Teddy slowly drifted away until all that was left was pain and darkness.

The dreams came and went. He heard people talking around him, and then they too were gone in the darkness.

Another picture flowed into his mind, and he was rolling with the ship. He felt a smile widen his mouth as spray struck his face. The clipper ship was racing over the tall waves. Down one and up another, pushed by a steady wind. These were the days that sometimes drove the memory of his dead parents from his mind. Porpoises rolled and leaped alongside while flying fish sailed from the froth-torn tops of the waves.

Thanks to Uncle Teddy, the past four years had been wonderful aboard the *Madeline*. He was second mate, destined to be a master with the company. But was that what he really wanted? At nineteen years of age, he had already been attacked by pirates, shipwrecked in the Pacific islands, and sailed into exotic ports too numerous to number. With all of this, then why was he still restless? *Restless,* he thought, *that's what I am,* and the blackness rolled over him again.

Somewhere in his bleak and pain-filled mind, he heard the judge come into his ship's cabin and ask how he was doing, but that would be impossible.

Jack started coughing. Coughing hard, and his eyes jerked opened to see a blurry man with a stethoscope around his neck. Jack tried to say something to the doctor, but all he could do was croak.

The doctor reached for a glass of water. With his other hand, he lifted Jack's head and held the glass to his lips. "Drink this, it'll help."

Jack took a sip, his mouth feeling like it was coated with hot desert sand. He tried to drink faster and started coughing again.

Doc Pratt held his head in place but pulled the glass away from his lips. "Easy. You don't want to rush it." He turned his head toward the door. "Martha, I need you."

Moments later she stepped into the doorway.

"What can I do, David?"

"Honey, would you get Judge Coleman? He asked to see Marshal Sage when he woke up." The doctor turned back to Jack.

The few drops of water down Jack's parched throat helped. He was able to croak, "Water."

Dr. Pratt returned the glass to Jack's mouth. "How are you feeling?"

Jack drank until the glass was empty, and leaned back on his pillow. He cleared his throat and made another attempt to talk. His voice had changed. It was raspy with a bit of coarseness in it. "Doc, I'm feeling like somebody tried to hang me, and I fell into a canyon."

He coughed a couple of times, made fists, and stretched his long arms above him, then, drawing an arc, extended them out to his sides. His shoulder felt better than it had since he dislocated it. Jack focused on the doctor's face, then he moved his head to view the open window. Outside the window, a desert wren was hopping along a mesquite limb. He could see the white stripe along the bird's eyes and the specks on its breast. His vision was better. Still a little blurry, but much better. He could actually see out his right eye. *I am feeling better,* he thought.

He nodded to the doctor. "Feeling better, Doc." He reached up with both hands and felt his eyes. The swelling was almost completely gone. He could feel the scab from the cut over his right eye, but at least the eye could be opened, and the vision was pretty good. "How'd I get here?"

The doctor, in the wingback chair, leaned forward and placed his forearms on his thighs, clasping his hands together. "That's an interesting story, Marshal."

Jack shook his head. "Call me Jack." He looked under the sheet. He was in a bed-shirt. A faint grin lifted the corners of his mouth. "Reckon you know me well enough to be on a first-name basis."

"Good, your sense of humor's still intact. That is borderline amazing after all you've been through.

"Jack, here's what we know. You were handed over to a rancher just outside town by Chief Victorio of the Chiricahua Apaches. He brought you in on a travois pulled by one of Rush's horses. Why he didn't kill you is beyond me, but here you are. I swear, I have never seen anyone as beat up as you were. And your neck, obviously somebody hanged you. I'm guessing you have a tale to beat all tales, and I'd love to hear it, including the story of those." The doctor pointed to the dresser next to the bed. On top sat three large gold nuggets and a quartz rock laced with gold.

"Doc, if I could talk you out of another glass of water, I'd be obliged. As far as the story, how about if I wait until the judge gets here, and I'll tell it once for everyone to hear."

The doctor filled Jack's glass with water. "You think you have the strength to hold it?"

Jack reached for the glass with his big right hand. Both arms were still a little sore, but they were nothing like they had been. His big fingers curled around the glass, and he brought it to his lips and began to drink. His throat was sore, both on the inside and out. Big scabs ringed his neck where the rope had torn skin away. When he swallowed, it felt like there was a lump in his throat, but everything seemed to go down alright. His mind drifted to Rush and his men laughing while he choked to death. A cold anger welled up inside him. It was going to be a pleasure to bring those men to justice, especially Elijah Rush.

Jack could hear the sound of the front door opening and closing, followed by heavy boots moving toward the bedroom. A moment later Judge Coleman and Marshal Hardwick entered the room, followed by Martha Pratt. The doctor rose. "I'll be right back."

The two men acknowledged the doctor with a nod and marched straight to Jack's bedside.

Judge Coleman extended his hand. "Welcome back, Jack. You gave us quite a scare."

Jack took the judge's hand. "Can't say I wasn't a little worried, myself."

Hardwick, wasting little time with pleasantries, ran his hand over his neck while staring at Jack. "Who did that to you?"

Jack was equally blunt. "Rush, two of his boys, and three others."

The doc returned with his wife and three additional straight-back wooden chairs. He placed them around the bed and pointed to the wingback chair. "Honey, why don't you go ahead and have a seat." He looked at Jack. "Alright with you?"

"Sure thing. I imagine you folks are the reason I'm still alive. I figure you've got just as much right, if not more, to hear my story as anyone else." He looked at Hardwick. "I'll answer your question first."

Jack began with the cowhands getting ropes on him. He told it to an enthralled audience. When he talked about the limb of the hanging tree breaking, Hardwick shook his head. "You are one lucky feller, Jack Sage."

Jack halted his story and thought about the marshal's statement. "You're partially right. I'm not lucky as far as getting into trouble. I seem to have done that a lot in my life, but I have been mighty lucky in getting out of it." He went on talking about his fall, the slanting canyon wall, hitting the boulder with his right shoulder, and managing to get into his little cave before one of Rush's gang could put a bullet in him.

He told of how he found the nuggets, following the arroyo to the gold vein, and making it out of the canyon. His luck continued when he found the two Rush hands had tied their horses right in front of where he climbed out of the canyon. The extra amazing part was they were in such a hurry to get to the women, they left their rifles in the scabbards, just for him.

Hardwick shook his head and uttered one word. "Lucky."

Jack continued, explaining about the two Apache women who had been captured by the two men of Rush's gang.

Judge Coleman asked, "What happened to those men?"

Jack turned to look at the judge. "Now what do you think happened to them, Judge? Those riders chased two Apache women and caused the mama to break her leg. I can just imagine what Victorio did to those two, and I figure they got what they deserved."

"You don't know what happened?"

"No, Judge, I don't. I passed out right after they found me. So I don't know what Victorio did to those fellas. Before I passed out, I did hear one scream. I'm guessing you don't have to worry about sending them to prison, though."

Hardwick, shaking his head, spoke up. "They messed with the wrong women. I'm tellin' you, they're dead, and they oughta count their lucky stars to have it over with. I imagine it lasted a lot longer than they wanted, and I guarantee it wasn't pleasant."

Jack said nothing.

Judge Coleman leaned forward. "What's your plan?"

Jack gave the judge a surprised look. "Same as it's always been. I plan on bringing the Rush bunch to justice."

The judge looked at Hardwick and back to Jack. "Even after what they've done to you? You're not a little concerned about your life?"

Jack's face hardened. "Are you asking me if I'm scared, Judge?" His cold gray eyes locked on the judge's face.

Judge Coleman's eyebrows lifted, and he spread his hands. "I wouldn't say scared, maybe a little more cautious?"

Jack said nothing and continued to stare at the judge.

Coleman cleared his throat. "There would be nothing wrong with a man feeling a bit more cautious after what you've been through."

Jack took a deep breath, his mending rib reminding him it wasn't healed yet. He exhaled. "Judge, there's a lot you don't know about me. I've covered many a mile and fought in a pile of battles where men have died. I don't turn tail and run if I receive a few scratches from a man who got lucky. His luck won't hold, and mine will change. Thanks to a few coincidences, his men were able to get a rope on me. They had their lucky chance, and they blew it. The next time, they might find themselves on the other end of Lady Luck's rope. If they do, I'll be there to throw and hogtie them. Am I going after Rush and his crew? Yep. Am I going to beat them? Yep. And when I'm done with them, I've got some gold to go after. Anything else?"

Hardwick leaned forward in his chair. "Next time, you'll be leading a posse."

Jack gave his head a single shake. "Nope."

Not used to being told no, Marshal Quinton Hardwick jerked back in his chair. "What do you mean, nope?"

"Just what I said. I work alone or with one other man. I don't ride with posses. You might as well send a telegraph message you're on your way as ride in a posse. No chance."

It was Hardwick's turn to look at the judge, who shrugged. The marshal turned þack to Jack. "If I tell you to take a posse, you'll take a posse."

"Listen to me, Hardwick. The judge hired me, you didn't. You were passed out on the floor of the saloon, unconscious from being pistol-whipped by Elijah Rush. The point is, I'm not taking a posse even if the judge tells me to."

Hardwick leaped to his feet. "I'm the United States Marshal for this territory. You'll do what I say, or I'll have your badge."

Jack was tired. He didn't know if he was more tired from his hanging and beating, or the railing of Hardwick, but he was tired. In fact he was ready to sleep. He pulled one of the stacked pillows from behind him and began to slide down in the bed. "I'm tired. My badge is on the dresser. Feel free to take it. I'm going to sleep."

His last vision was the red face of Hardwick.

Jack knew he would get Rush and his gang, but he wouldn't do it with anybody's posse, not today, not any day. With a satisfied smile on his lips, his heavy eyelids slammed shut, and he slid deep into a welcome, restful sleep.

11

Jack tried on the set of clothes Martha Pratt, Dr. Pratt's wife, had purchased for him. She had paid with one of the smaller nuggets while the clerk constantly questioned her over the source of the gold. Jack smiled at the thought of anyone interrogating Martha Pratt. She was an attractive, kind, and pleasant woman, but she was also as stubborn as Stonewall, his mule. He had chuckled when she told him the tale. The clerk had no chance against her. He looked at his old boots. *Old,* he thought, *I haven't had them for four months, and they're worn out.* He picked one up and plied the leather top. These were the best boots he had ever owned, and Rush's bunch had ruined them. He felt the cold anger in his chest and could feel his scalp tingle, a dead giveaway of his fury.

He took a deep breath and relaxed. His rib gave a slight twinge, but nothing serious. It was healing fast. It had been almost three weeks since he dove into Hangman's Canyon, at least that was what he had named it. *Appropriate, too*, he thought.

He wiggled his toes. The new boots were tight. He'd have to ride through a river and let them get soaked on his feet. That would adjust them to his size. The other clothes fit fine. He tied the silk green and black bandanna around his neck. The wound was still livid, and a few scabs remained in places, but it was feeling much better.

Jack's voice had improved, but it had lost its mellow tone. Now it was gritty and harsh. *Maybe it'll get better,* he thought. *The doc says it will, but if I'm stuck with it, so be it. At least my eyesight is nearing normal.* Jack wasn't a worrier, but his vision had been a real concern for him. In his line of business even a small change could spell disaster, but now, his eyes, especially the severely injured right eye, had been getting better each day that passed. His perfect vision had almost returned, for which he was thankful. His remaining three regrets were the loss of his San Francisco Stetson, the destruction of his boots, and the theft of his two custom-made .36-caliber Remington New Model Police revolvers. Other than throwing a slug a little smaller than he preferred, they were perfect weapons. The bullet went where he pointed, and they had never misfired. They were weapons a man could depend on. It was a dark day when he lost them.

Jack snorted in disgust. *I didn't lose them. They were stolen by a two-bit thief.* His goal today was to take a stroll around town, check his strength, his endurance, pick up some more gear, and buy himself at least one more revolver. He also wanted to see his animals and check on Thunder.

The big horse had made it back from Jack's hanging without getting captured. Tiny had come by to tell Jack about the gray. When he came into the stable, he had trotted straight for Smokey, Pepper, and Stonewall. Tiny said it was like old home week. Upon hearing the commotion, he had gone into the barn from his office, and there Thunder stood, still saddled, rifle and saddlebags strapped tight. Thunder had some deep scratches on his neck, back, and across the saddle where he must have carried a hungry mountain lion for a ways, but other than those marks, he was fine.

Jack's thoughts swung back to his revolvers. The Colt he had taken from Rush's man worked fine. The fella had taken good care of it, but it didn't really fit his needs. It was too long for one thing, so he'd need at least one, and maybe two if he found the right weapons.

One of the sheriff's deputies, on occasion, had stopped by to see how Jack was doing. He was the one who had helped him during the altercation in town when Jack had winged Cooper.

Today, the deputy had stopped by to walk him over to a gunsmith's shop. He said the man was magic with weapons. He also said he had an assortment to choose from and suggested Jack might find exactly what he wanted. Jack, needing to get outside and never a man to refuse a trip to a gun shop, was ready when the deputy showed up at the doctor's home. At the knock, Jack walked to the door and called to Martha, "I've got it. Don't bother yourself." Opening it, he saw Deputy Billy Brice. The deputy's tall, peaked, black Stetson contrasted with a mass of thick honey-blond hair. He flashed a wide grin to Jack, exposing a perfect set of white teeth. Billy, a slow-talking friendly fella, liked his hair. He seldom wore his hat, most often carrying it in one hand or the other. With his blue eyes and wide smile, Deputy Brice never had a problem enlisting the company of the fairer sex to attend any dance, picnic, or carnival that might be in town.

"You about ready?" hatless Billy Brice asked.

Jack liked the boy. He thought of him as a boy since Blond Billy was at least twelve years younger than Jack, and the boy sometimes acted twenty years younger, in Jack's estimation. "That hat's to wear, Billy."

Deputy Billy's grin widened. "Shoot, Marshal, I can't mess up my hair. What would the girls think?"

"They might think your head's where your hat belongs," Jack replied in his gritty voice, stepping off the porch and moving carefully down the three steps. He was about four inches taller than the deputy, but the boy stood straight, and with his wide shoulders and sun-darkened face, he looked taller, and the tall head of blond hair didn't hurt either.

The two walked along the street, staying clear of the walkway so the ladies could pass. It was a beautiful fall afternoon in Silver City, and the population who could be was out enjoying it. Every time a woman, young or old, passed, she would light up and give Billy a wide smile. He'd smile back and say something complimentary. "Morning, Mrs. Wells. That blue dress looks like it was cut right out of the sky," or "Morning, Nancy, your hair looks more lovely every day." He had something to say to everyone, even the grandmother he met on the street. "Morning, Mrs. Thomas, it's always nice to see such a lovely lady out on a day like this."

Mrs. Thomas beamed at Deputy Billy. "You've got a sweet tongue, Billy, but you've always been a sweetie. Tell your ma hi for me."

Jack shook his head. "Do you have any end to your gab? You oughta be ashamed of yourself."

The boy turned to look up at Jack. "Marshal, it's no sin to be kind to folks. That's what I try to do. My ma taught me when you brighten the day of someone else, you've given them about the best gift there is."

Jack nodded. "Well, I'll say you've got a mighty smart ma. Now where the blue blazes is this gunsmith you've been talking about?"

Billy angled toward a door they were nearing. "This is it. What this feller don't know about guns, nobody knows. He takes off-the-shelf weapons, tightens and smooths them out to where there's no rough spots anywhere, and makes 'em feel custom built. He works magic. Why, he knows guns like a fisherman knows his favorite fishing hole."

The bell jingled as Jack and Billy stepped through the door. A tall man, looking younger than his gray hair would indicate, came through a curtain hung over the back entryway. He had

Jack's height but was much slimmer. Jack spotted the man's type immediately. He had worked with men like this fella in the Legion and in the war. The gray-haired man's alert eyes and manner gave him away. He missed nothing, his eyes constantly moving. He didn't have a problem making eye contact, but he continued to clear the area through the windows even as he talked. *This man,* Jack thought, *was a sharpshooter somewhere, for a long time, because the look hasn't faded.*

"Jack," Billy said, "this is Andrew McClintock, and I guarantee he can fix you up."

The man's face broke into a sincere but understated smile. He extended his hand. "Hi, Marshal Sage, call me Andy."

Jack took the man's hand and felt a firm, but not overpowering grip. "I'm Jack to you, Andy, reckon you've seen the bear."

A portion of Andy's smile faded. "Yep, I saw a bit of the war. How can I 'fix you up,' as Billy said?"

Jack patted the Colt in his holster. "I'm sure this is a fine weapon, but I never took much to Mr. Colt's products, too fragile for me. I like something a little more sturdy, like a Remington."

Andy's smile transformed into a wide grin. "I guarantee you'll be in an argument in a heartbeat if you say that in any saloon."

Billy patted the Colt in his holster. "That's for sure."

Jack held up his hands. "Alright, but you know what I mean."

Andy nodded. "I do." He walked out from behind the counter so it wouldn't block his view of Jack. "Let your hands hang down by your sides."

Jack did as he was told. The gunsmith, his left arm across his waist, cradling the elbow of his right, stroked his chin with his right hand. "H-m-m-m, you've got long arms. Hold out your hands."

Jack held his hands in front of him, palms up. His old leather gloves had done an excellent job of protecting him in Hangman's Canyon, but there were still several gashes carrying scabs.

Andy nodded. "Heard about your little escapade with our outlaw rancher. Guess you got those then."

Jack dropped his hands. "I did. So does the whole town know?"

Andy returned behind the counter. "Pretty much. Maybe the town drunk hasn't heard yet, but I guess everyone else has."

Jack shook his head. "I guess there's not much chance of keeping anything quiet in Silver City."

"Nope." Andy winked at Jack. "Once Billy finds out, the whole town pretty much knows."

Billy had been looking at a hand-tooled holster hanging on the wall. He dropped it, letting it swing back and forth, and turned to Andy. "Now, wait a minute. I ain't told a soul about Jack. That was that loud-mouth judge bragging on him. He was the one spreadin' all that gossip around."

Andy grinned at the younger man. "Easy, Billy, I was just funnin' you. We know the only people you told were the ladies."

Jack couldn't help but laugh.

Billy sputtered for a second, then spit out, "And everybody knows you're full of it, Andy McClintock."

"Aye, lad," Andy said, "that is probably true." His face turned serious. "Jack, I understand you lost everything when you were grabbed by Rush?"

"Not quite, my horse Thunder made it back with my 1866 Winchester and supplies. He's my next stop. I haven't seen him since I returned. However, I did lose my revolvers. They'd been with me since shortly before the war ended. They were .36-caliber Remington New Model Police with the three-and-a-half-inch barrel. They were new factory models my gunsmith, he was a friend of my family in Virginia, rebuilt. They had the smoothest actions I've ever felt."

Andy nodded as he listened. "So you liked the .36 caliber?"

Jack heard yelling from outside the shop, turned, and watched a muleskinner driving his wagon through town.

Evidently, several of his mules were being less than cooperative. He watched until the wagon passed, mulling Andy's question over in his mind, then turned back to the gunsmith. "I'll tell you. I liked the weapons. With my big hands, I could reach the hammer when I held the revolver in firing position. It wasn't so on the bigger Remingtons or Colts. Oh, in the recoil, it was easy to thumb the hammer back for the next shot, but it was nice holding the little .36. It felt good." Andy started to speak again, but Jack, holding up a hand, stopped him. "I know, you asked about the caliber. I'd like to have a heavier bullet, but I'd hate to give up the lighter weight of my Remingtons. I could shuck them pretty fast."

Andy, while listening closely to Jack, had bent over and was rummaging through several boxes beneath the counter. "I have something that might just suit your needs." He rose suddenly and turned to the gunrack, selecting an 1866 Winchester Carbine. Lifting it from the rack, he opened the action and laid it across the counter.

Jack glanced at the Winchester. It was a nice-looking rifle, but he had one just like it. "I don't need a rifle, Andy. I need revolvers, and ones that I like."

"Don't get prickly, big fella, just bear with me." He continued shuffling boxes beneath the counter. "Ah, here they are." The gunsmith lifted a box and placed it next to the rifle. He opened it, removed an attractive, dark wooden presentation case, and set it on the counter. Flipping the wooden case around to face Jack, he lifted the lid. Inside were two Smith & Wesson .44-caliber Americans.

Jack was surprised to see the barrel length. *Those barrels can't be over four inches,* he thought. *They're larger weapons, but with the loss of the long barrel, they just might work.*

"Pick one up," Andy said, "and push the latch on the top of the frame."

Jack hefted one. It was heavier than one of his Remingtons,

but not by a lot. He liked the feel, even with the heavier weight. "I've seen a few of these, saw 'em in the war, but the only ones I ever saw had an eight-inch barrel, way too long."

"Yep. If you'll notice, the barrel slot in the case is about four inches longer than the barrels. I've done a little work on these two. After I finished, I brought 'em out front but left 'em in the box. I haven't been able to make up my mind to sell or keep them." He picked up a box of cartridges from the counter, grabbed the remaining revolver from the case, and began loading it. "Load that one up. Stuff it full. You don't have to carry it on an empty cylinder for fear of blowing your leg off, like the Colt, and the Remington if you're not careful."

Jack pushed the release latch on the revolver. The weapon, hinged at the bottom front of the receiver, dropped open, and a cogwheel at the center of the cylinder extended. It would extract all six of the fired cartridges at one time. He looked at Andy. "That would speed up reloading considerably."

"It does. That's what you're going to find out. Load up and come on." He glanced at Billy. "Bring the box of cartridges, and I might even let you shoot a few."

"Can't pass that up." Billy leaned on the counter, waiting for Jack to load his weapon.

Jack took six cartridges from the box and dropped them into their respective chambers. Once loaded, he snapped the revolver closed, pulled the Colt from his holster, and handed it to Billy. "Hold that, would you?"

Billy took it and followed the two other men through the curtained passage into the gunsmith's workshop and out the back door.

Behind the shop, Andy had set up a range of sorts. At fifty yards, he had built a backstop of dirt and rocks. It would keep most bullets from traveling any farther. High shots would disappear into the desert. At ten yards, he had set up a couple of paper targets. They were simple, with only a two-inch bullseye in the middle of the brown paper.

Jack had dropped the Smith into the holster. The fit wasn't perfect, but it would do for the short term. He stepped out, looked at the target and then at Andy.

"You can do whatever you want. Aim and shoot, draw and shoot, I don't care. The main thing is to get the feel of the weapon and the action."

Jack decided to draw, not the rapid draw needed to save his life, but just draw and fire from the hip. His hand flashed down and found the butt of the new revolver. Hand and revolver rose to hip level while his big thumb was pulling the hammer to full cock, and the barrel was rotating to level. The weapon fired, once, twice, three times. Three holes appeared touching the bullseye, one at twelve o'clock, one at nine o'clock, and one at three.

Without halting, Jack brought the Smith to eye level, thumbed the hammer back and fired three times. This time, three holes appeared in the center of the target, making a nice cloverleaf with all three touching. He brought the weapon down, pushed the lever on the top, and jerked it open. Six empty cartridges flew out. *I like that,* Jack thought. *It makes reloading so much faster.* He turned to look at Andy.

The gunsmith nodded. "Not bad for a man who's been shooting a lighter weapon and has gone through what you have. I doubt you're yet at a hundred percent. Why, most people couldn't shoot that good when they're feelin' their best." He glanced at Billy. "You wanta shoot?"

Billy shook his head. "I'm not sure I want to follow that, but yeah, I'd like to try one of those out."

Andy handed the deputy the Smith he had been carrying and took the Colt. Billy's first shots were from the hip at the target Jack had shot.

Not bad, Jack thought. He watched the shots scatter around the center. There was no grouping unless you called the six rounds a group, which would then make it about eleven inches. If the younger man had been firing for his life, any of his shots would have put down his opponent, though for sure they would have needed at least one more to put them completely out of commission.

Billy and Andy traded weapons. Billy, looking a bit embarrassed, said, almost sounding like an apology, "Not quite as good as you, Jack."

Jack shook his head. "Don't be apologetic about your shooting. Any of those would've put the gunman down. You just need a little more practice. You've got to remember, I've been doing this a lot longer than you, and I've had a lot more targets shooting back. Work on it. You'll get better."

Andy piped up, "That's right, Billy. You're way better than average, but you can improve." A mischievous look came into the man's eyes. "Of course, you might have to give up some of your time with the ladies."

"That's asking too much," Billy said. "Let's shoot some more."

12

J ack had fired both of the Smiths, also allowing Billy to blast a few rounds. Even with the minimal amount of shooting, Jack could already see an improvement in the younger man's targeting. They finished the fifty rounds in the box and retraced their steps to the gunsmith's showroom. Once inside the gun shop, Jack handed Andy his Smith and retrieved the Colt from Billy. "I like them. How much? I'll also need holsters."

"Before we talk about the money, let me show you one more thing." Andy handed Jack a round from the .44 Henry.

Jack mentally kicked himself. He hadn't even noticed the ammunition he was loading into the weapons. Of course it was .44 Henry rounds he'd been firing in the two handguns. As much to himself as to Andy, Jack said, "These revolvers shoot the same thing as the Winchester and the Henry."

"Now they do. I reworked the chambers and barrels on those two handguns. They'll fire Henry ammunition all day long."

Billy spoke up. "Why'd you do that?"

Andy shrugged. "I'm a gunsmith. It seemed like a good idea. I waited for Winchester to catch on, but they haven't yet, and a lot of soldiers and cowhands have mentioned how much better it'd be if their pistols and rifles fired the same stuff. I figured I'd give it a try. These are the first two. I've retooled my equipment, and I'm ready to get started. I'll be converting round-ball Colt and Remington handguns here pretty soon."

Jack pointed at the two revolvers lying on the counter. "That's all well and good, Andy, but how much are those?"

The gunsmith looked a little sheepish. "They're kinda expensive. I spent a bunch of hours on each one. If you came in and bought a new, unmodified Smith, it would be forty-three dollars. But with the time I put in, I'll have to charge you sixty bucks apiece. That doesn't include the leather or ammunition."

Billy let out a long whistle. "That's a bunch of money, Jack. Maybe you oughta stick with the round-ball guns. They're a lot cheaper."

Andy nodded. "Billy's right, Jack. I've got a Colt over here that'll match the one you have, and it's only twenty-four dollars, big difference."

Jack picked up one of the Smith and Wessons, pulled the hammer back, and spun the cylinder. With the four-inch barrel, the weapon balanced perfectly in his hand, and he'd quickly adjust to the slight change in weight. He laid it gently back on the counter, alongside its companion, and looked directly at the gunsmith. "No, Andy, you've put in a lot of work on these Smiths, and besides being exquisite weapons, the fact they shoot the same round as my rifle is crucial. This is a more than fair deal." He gave an emphatic nod. "I want them both, but I'll need new holsters for these babies."

Andy grinned and left the room. He knocked the curtain out of his way, disappeared into the workshop, and called from the back, "I've got just the thing. Had old Mr. Martinez make it for me. I swear he must've pictured you."

He walked back in carrying a rig that was one wide belt with two holsters slung, a bit lower than normal, on each side and handed it to Jack. The big man took it, examining the hand-tooled leather belt and the rearing mustangs engraved on the holsters. It was heavy for a gun belt, but the main belt had loops for ammunition all around except for where the holsters were attached. *I could carry almost a box of ammunition on the belt,* Jack thought. He fingered the loops and looked across the counter at Andy. "This is a great gun belt. Did he make it to order?"

Andy was shaking his head. "No, I told him to make a belt and holster for two guns that would shoot metal cartridges. I had no idea he would come up with this. I was pretty mad when I first saw it. I mean, it's pretty, but the holsters are so low. He just smiled and told me to take it. He's done all of my leather work, so I paid him and took it, figuring I'd take the loss." Still shaking his head, he added, "And here you are. Go ahead, try it on."

Jack unfastened the buckle of his gun belt, wrapped the belt around the Colt and holster, and laid it on the counter. He picked up the new rig, swung it around his narrow hips and, pulling the tongue tight, fastened the belt. Taking the shortened Smith and Wessons, he slid one after another into their respective holsters. They rode a little heavier, and the ammunition in the belt would increase the weight, but he didn't think it would be enough to present a problem.

Andy nodded. "Try the guns. They'll slide out of those holsters like a couple of greased pigs."

Jack did as the gunsmith suggested. The man was right. They slid easily in and out, and after several months of treatment and their shaping the holsters, they'd get even better. The revolvers also sat a little lower than his old ones had. Now, as his hands came up in a draw, the butts of the weapons were right there, ready to be grasped. He looked up from the holsters. "This is a great rig, Andy. Mr. Martinez knew what he was doing. I swear they come out easier than my Remingtons did." He felt around the loops on the belt in front of and behind the holsters and thought, *No more worries about round ball, and the cartridges work in both my rifle and the revolvers.*

"Alright, Andy. Take the Colt in trade, add five hundred rounds of .44 Henry, and give me a total."

Andy let out a low whistle. "Five hundred, sounds like a young war."

"I need a little practice. Figure I'll work on that a mite before leaving. Now give me a total, and I'll be on my way."

The gunsmith took out a pad and began figuring. He finally added the numbers and turned the pad toward Jack and Billy. Billy's eyes almost bugged out at the amount.

Jack pulled a bag from his vest pocket and counted out eight twenty-dollar gold pieces. "Will that do?"

"Just right," Andy said. "You have any problem with those Smiths, bring 'em back, and I'll fix 'em, or anything else, no charge."

"Much obliged. Just let me have two of the boxes now, and I'll pick up the remaining eight later." Andy dropped two boxes of .44 Henry on the counter. Jack opened one and began to reload both revolvers and fill the loops on the gun belt. When he was finished, he had emptied the box—thirty-eight rounds on the belt and all the loops were filled. He thought, *Mr. Martinez knew exactly what he was doing.* Jack slid the empty box back to Andy, picked up the full one, nodded, and started for the door, Billy following.

"Marshal, you ever need any help, I'm available, especially for the long-range stuff."

Jack looked back at Andy. The gunsmith held his gaze. Jack gave him a nod and pushed the door open, striding outside.

Billy stepped up next to Jack. "Andy's never volunteered to help anyone, not the sheriff or the U.S. Marshal. You're the first. Why you reckon that is?"

Jack checked the street and buildings in both directions.

"Reckon I need some clothes and a hat. I can't walk around hatless all day, like you."

Billy, ignoring Jack's comment on his penchant for not wearing his hat, pointed up the street. "Well, then I imagine Silver City's finest is what you're lookin' for. The Southwest Mercantile is the place for you. It'll have a big assortment of hats, and clothes if you'd like to add to your wardrobe. I've gotta check in with the office. Never know when the sheriff might have something for me to handle."

"See you later, Billy. Thanks for your help."

The two separated, and Jack made his way to the mercantile, where he picked up a few clothes and a new hat. It was another gray Stetson. He seemed to gravitate to gray, though he did like green, but had never seen a green hat, nor would he buy one if he had. He'd leave it for an Irishman. He smiled at the thought.

He stepped out the door of the mercantile, adjusted his new hat, and with his newly purchased clothes in a wrapped and tied bag under his left arm, he started for the doc's place. He had wanted to stop by Tiny's livery and see his animals, but he was tired. His energy hadn't completely returned. This would not be the day for Thunder, Smokey, Pepper or Stonewall, maybe tomorrow.

Passing the Jolly Rancher Saloon, his boot heel caught the corner of a large flagstone. He stumbled forward.

Simultaneously, a rifle cracked.

He felt the bullet pass through the crown of his hat. Papa had taught him not to swear, and except for a couple of extreme situations, he did pretty well, but right now, he felt like swearing. Whoever it was with that rifle had put a bullet straight through his brand-new hat.

He ducked around a corner of the nearest building, whipped out a .44, and eased back to where he could see. Nothing, the streets were cleared completely. Everyone had disappeared. With all the bullets flying over the past month, people were getting gun-shy. He waited to see if there would be any movement or anything that might indicate where the bullet had come from. When he could see nothing, he stepped out from behind the building.

He saw Billy and the sheriff step from their office. Billy had a rifle in his hands. Farther down the street, Marshal Hardwick moved into the street, carrying a shotgun. When he saw Jack, he started toward him, but stopped upon reaching the sheriff and Billy. They stood talking. Jack, satisfied the gunman had taken off, turned back inside the mercantile. He bought another hat just like the one that had been holed. Leaving the one with a hole on his head, he carried the bag under his left arm and his new hat in his left hand. Hardwick was still talking to the sheriff and Billy when Jack again came out of the Silver City Mercantile. He headed toward them.

Drawing near the group, Hardwick called out, "Did you see who that shot was meant for?"

Jack said nothing. Upon reaching them, he pointed to the hole in his new hat.

Billy's face split into a wide grin, showing off his perfect teeth. "That's why I don't wear my hat, Jack. You should take up my habit. It would've saved you buying another one." He pointed to the hat in Jack's hand.

"Funny. Did any of you see anything?"

All three shook their heads. Hardwick, his eyes still searching the streets and buildings, said, "You figure it was one of the Rush bunch?"

Jack shrugged. "Your guess is as good as mine. Nobody saw anything. There's no way to tell. I've left some unhappy people along my trail, so it could've been anyone, including Rush or one of his people."

Hardwick continued, "What are you going to do?"

"Right now, I'm heading back to the doc's. I'm thinking on my next move. I might want to hire someone to go with me. Is that a problem?"

"I do the hiring and firing in this territory, Sage. If you want me to hire some people to go after Rush with you, tell me, and I'll get it done."

Jack hated bureaucracies, no matter how big or small. It was one of the reasons he had been hesitant to hire on with the Marshal Service. If it was part of the government, it was going to be a pain to work with. All he wanted to do was hire one man, maybe two, and he didn't need Hardwick sticking his nose into it. "How about if I take care of it?"

Hardwick motioned with his head. "Come on down to my office, and we'll talk about it."

Jack nodded to the sheriff and Billy and followed Hardwick. Inside, he could see it wasn't much of an office. A desk, a window, and three chairs, with a rifle rack behind the desk. The rack held two Winchesters, a Spencer, and two shotguns. There were several cabinet drawers beneath the rack. Jack figured they held ammunition for all of the weapons plus maybe a few extra handguns.

Hardwick eyed his new holsters and revolvers. "Restocking?"

Jack ignored his question. "Why can't I hire a couple of men on my own?"

Hardwick dropped into the chair behind his desk and leaned back. "The reason you can't, Deputy Marshal Sage, is because you're the deputy and I'm the marshal. When you're the marshal, you can do the hiring." Hardwick's eyebrows climbed up his high forehead. "You say a couple of men? Just a moment ago you were only talking about one. Now you've doubled the number. We're not made out of money, you know."

Jack set his new purchases on the edge of Hardwick's desk and leaned forward. "Look, I didn't ask for this job. In fact, I didn't want it. I came up here to look for gold, and—"

"From what I hear, you found time to locate yourself a strike instead of pursuing Rush."

Jack's scalp began to tingle. He considered yanking the badge from his vest and tossing it into the marshal's lap but controlled his impulse. He did reach up and yank the bandanna from around his neck, exposing the scabs and livid scars. "Did you also hear I managed to get hanged by Rush and his gang?"

The marshal dropped his arrogant facade. "Yeah, I did hear that. Sorry it happened. That shouldn't happen to any man." He waited a few moments and opened the top desk drawer. "If you need to hire a couple of men, just do it, and send me their names. You can tell 'em they'll be making the same as you." He paused and pointed a finger at Jack. "No more than two." Then he slid two deputy badges across the desk.

Jack caught the badges and dropped them into his pocket. "Why the change of mind?"

Hardwick leaned back. "I'm leaving town with the judge, today, headed back to Socorro. I won't be around to do any hiring, so you'll have to do it."

So much for becoming reasonable, Jack thought.

"The judge has a few trials lined up over Socorro way and needs a marshal along to take care of everything, so I guess that's me." His perpetual frown deepened. "For two cents I'd hang this job up myself."

Jack rose and picked up his packages. "Have a nice trip." He turned to head out the door.

"Hold on. When you hire whoever you hire, tell the bank. They'll take care of their pay. I'll be authorizing only two men."

"Is that it?"

"Yeah, that's it. Git out of here."

Jack turned and pushed through the door. As far as he was concerned, he couldn't get out of the office quick enough. Leaving the marshal's office, he headed for the doctor's place. He figured he was over most of his bad injuries, but an awful weakness had come over him. *I just need a little more rest*, he thought. *I'd best be moving back into the hotel where all my things are, but I'll do that tomorrow. I'm feeling mighty tired.*

He pushed past the doc's front door to be met by Martha Pratt. She was standing there looking at him with the same look he remembered receiving from his mama. Her hand was raised, and a slim finger pointed at him. "Mr. Sage, you haven't recovered from your wounds yet. Give me those packages." Her hands shot out, and she yanked away his new hat and package of clothes, and in a raised voice, she called, "David."

A moment later the doctor stepped into the parlor and exclaimed, "Jack, look at you." He turned to Martha. "Get him a bowl of the soup you made for lunch, and several slices of corn-bread. He's about to drop." He grabbed Jack by his arm. "Come in here, and get in bed. You shouldn't be overdoing it like this. Your body has had a lot of damage. It takes time to recover."

Jack started to argue that he was feeling fine, but he really wasn't. In fact, sitting down sounded really good. "Look, Doc, why don't I just go into the kitchen and sit at the table. I appreciate your hospitality, but I've been here way too long. I've got work to do."

The doctor shook his head. "You haven't been here long enough, Jack. I see those new guns. You're planning on pulling out and going after Rush, but I'm telling you, your body won't take it. You leave tomorrow, and you'll be down in the trail before the day is done. Listen to me. I know what I'm talking about." He had led Jack back into the bedroom where he was staying. There was a mirror on the dresser. Passing it, Dr. Pratt pointed with his free hand. "Look at yourself."

Jack turned his head to look in the mirror. The first thing he noticed was his pallor. He looked like a corpse on its feet. His skin was washed-out and flat, lifeless. The shooting today, the exertion from leaping behind the building, the adrenaline, it had all sucked his energy like a dust devil sucking up dust. Next he saw his beat-up face, the healed and still healing cuts and scratches. He looked worse than he ever had after a fight, and his eyes. Not the areas around his eyes where he had taken the blows from his fall, but the gray eyes themselves. This was the first time he had really looked since returning. His eyes didn't have the bright, clear look they normally had. They were dull gray, like a cloudy sky before a snowfall. He'd never seen them like this, not even after he'd lost his wife and son. He leaned a little more on the doctor's support. "Maybe you're right, Doc. That fella in the mirror looks pretty bad."

"Let me get you into bed, Jack. Martha will bring you soup. It'll help, but you still need to rest. You're pushing yourself too hard, too soon."

Jack sat on the edge of the bed while the doctor pulled his boots off, then removed his gun belt. "Doc, I can't stay here. I need to get back to my hotel room. I can't put you folks out any longer. Anyway, I've got a job to finish."

"Nonsense, as far as moving to the hotel, it's easier for us to take care of you here, and Rush will still be there when your body has healed."

Jack knew the doctor was right. He leaned over and fell into bed. He felt the doctor lift his legs. He straightened them and closed his eyes. He'd eat the soup later.

13

Jack stomped into his boots. There was a fire roaring in the bedroom fireplace and snow blowing against the windows. The day before, he had moved most of his things back to his hotel room, except for his rifle and saddlebags, which he still had, thanks to Thunder. He stood and swung his gun belt around his waist, fastened it, and checked both weapons were free and easy. He had purchased a Bowie knife, which was also looped on his gun belt. He felt like a new man.

Dr. Pratt had been right. The extra week had made a huge difference. Gazing into the mirror, he saw a completely different man than the one he had seen eight days earlier. His skin, though it had faded some from being inside, looked healthy, not pasty the way it had, but his eyes were the big difference. They looked alive. The eyes that had stared at him earlier looked like the eyes of a dying man. Today, they were bright. He could even see a little humor in them.

He nodded his head. He was back. Maybe he wasn't a hundred percent, but he was close, and his eyesight had completely returned. *All I need is a little fresh mountain air,* Jack thought and turned to look out the window. Snowflakes were flying at the glass and sticking around the edges. With the first storm, the temperature had plummeted. He chuckled to himself. *I wasn't planning on it being quite that fresh. But we'll be fine. Smokey and Stonewall have picked up enough fat lazing around the stable to keep them warm as toast.*

He picked up his rifle and saddlebags, relieved by the weight of his remaining stake. If Thunder had been caught by the Rush gang, or hadn't found his way back to Tiny's, Jack would be broke, but the big horse had come through. For that, Jack was going to let him rest in the nice warm stable. It was Smokey's turn to travel, and he knew the big grulla was ready.

He had one stop to make before riding out. First he had to say goodbye to the Pratt family. Because of them, he was alive. They had taken care of his every need when he first arrived, and refused to let him leave before his body was healed. He owed them more than he could repay.

Jack looked around the room that had been home for several weeks. *Yes, I owe you folks a lot,* Jack thought, *and I pay my debts.* He had tried to figure out how much he should pay them. He started with the charge for a hotel room for the same length of time, and added three meals a day, but that didn't begin to cover what they had done. His two new guns, along with the holsters and first batch of ammunition, had cost almost two hundred bucks. Surely Doc Pratt and Martha deserved more for saving his life. He still owed Tiny, and the thousands of dollars he'd made with the first herd he had trailed to Missouri was running low, but he had enough to pay what he owed and leave him with a bit of a pad. He laid four fifty-dollar greenbacks on the dresser and placed five double eagles across the top of them. Three hundred dollars wasn't enough for what they did, but it'd do for now.

He picked up his saddlebags and rifle and headed for the parlor. Doc Pratt and Martha were sitting next to each other on the brocade love seat. They both rose when he came into the room. "Reckon I can't begin to thank you two enough for everything you've done for me." The doctor started to say something, and Jack held up his hand. "Let me finish, Doc.

"I'm beholden to you. If it weren't for your care, I'm convinced the dirt above me would be getting covered by that fresh snow out there. Thanks." He looked at Martha. "And thank you, ma'am. You've gone way past kind. Why, when the peaches come back in, I may swing by for a taste of your fine peach pie." He looked at the doctor again. "Doc, if you or Martha ever need any help, get word to me. I'll drop everything and come a-running. Don't forget that."

He saw tears trying to slip from Martha's eyes. Her lips spread into the kind smile she was capable of showing. "Oh, Jack, you don't have to wait until then. Come by anytime. I have plenty of canned peaches."

The doctor extended his hand and said, as Jack took it, "We just helped, Jack. Any normal man would have died. You are exceptionally strong. Rush doesn't know what he's in for."

Martha sniffed. "Take care of yourself, and Jack, you shouldn't be leaving in this horrible weather. You'll catch your death of cold, and after we spent so much time getting you well."

They all laughed. Martha gave Jack a hug. He looked at them one more time and stepped out the door. The cold northwest wind slammed into him, and he pulled his hat tight to his head. There had been plenty of time for him to modify this hat, and the leather string hung beneath his chin, just in case the wind tried to separate them.

He turned toward Hank Marsden's office, the wind and snow whipping at his face. His long heavy wool coat felt good. It would take a greater wind than this to cut through the tight-weaved wool, though even through his leather chaps, he could feel the chill slicing at him.

He had met with Hank earlier, while he was healing. The two

of them had discussed his discovery and then made a deal, Jack partnering with the successful miner and prospector. They called in Maynard Womack, the attorney who had prosecuted Jasper Rush, to draw up their agreement. Their split was seventy percent to Hank, twenty-five percent to Jack, and five percent to the Pratts. Hank had been a little surprised at the amount he gave the Pratts, but Jack reminded the miner how the couple had saved his life. *Hank is a good man,* Jack thought. *He's hit one bonanza, and now it looks like he might have another.*

A horseman raced past Jack, flogging his animal. The horse looked almost ready to drop. Jack watched the man pull up in front of the sheriff's office, leap from the bay, and dash into the office. Jack had planned on stopping by Hank's office and discussing when the miner would check out the claim, but instead he turned and headed across the street to find out the problem. He wanted to get after Rush, but he was a lawman, and it looked like someone was in trouble.

Jack pushed the door open and stepped inside just in time to hear the man excitedly talking to the sheriff, whose right leg, covered in a cast from ankle to hip, was propped up on a chair.

"Dead, I'm tellin' ya. They're all dead. Every last one of 'em. The woman, too. They'd either been shot, had arrows stickin' in 'em, or both. The stage was left burnin', and the mules were taken." The man's voice rose, and his arms waved. "You've got to git after them Injuns. Git the army. Victorio is on the warpath, and nobody's safe. I'm tellin' ya. Nobody!" The man's voice had been rising until the last words were shouted.

Jack nodded to Billy, who was standing in the doorway of the jail entrance.

Sheriff Beasley pointed to a chair. "Sit down, Thomas. If they're all dead, there's no sense leaping after them in this storm. The bodies will keep in this cold weather." The sheriff glanced at Jack. "Howdy, Marshal. Glad to see you up and about. Looks like you picked a nasty day to be out."

Jack nodded and said nothing.

Thomas Chase remained standing. He turned and saw Jack. "Marshal, you've got to do something. Git the army. Victorio's on the loose. He's done killed all the folks on the stage and burnt it up. A plain horrible sight."

Jack watched the man's agitation increasing. "Don't you have a ranch down that way, Mr. Chase?"

"Yeah, Marshal, I surely do. Got me a wife and four kids out there. All they got with 'em are our two hired hands. Victorio could kill 'em all. We need to do something, and do it now."

"Mr. Chase, Sheriff Beasley and I will come up with something soon. Right now, you've delivered your message, and your lathered horse is standing outside freezing to death. Why don't you take him down to Tiny's, get him a good rubdown and feed, and we'll take care of this."

"But—"

"Mr. Chase." Jack's voice sharpened. "You go on. We're not going to rush half-cocked out there. You know what the weather's like. Now you go on and take care of your horse."

Jack's sharp tone had jerked the man out of his frenzy. "You're right, sorry. Toby's a fine horse. He could be freezing. I was thinking of my family. I guess I got a little worked up."

Jack responded, his voice more understanding. "You did right, Mr. Chase. You've got a legitimate reason to be upset. We'll figure out what we need to do and get on with it. You'd best be on your way. You can check back with the sheriff later."

Thomas Chase nodded and looked at the sheriff. "You'll let me know what you're gonna do? I wanta be of help. I can go with you."

The sheriff gave a slow nod. "We sure will, Thomas. Now you go ahead on."

Chase pulled the door open just as the Wells Fargo agent was reaching for the latch. He stepped past the agent, and Arlo Fetter pushed inside.

Fetter shoved the door closed against the wind. "Slade Jenkins just brought me word someone was in here yelling about the stage. What's happened to it?"

The sheriff looked at Jack, who nodded back at him. He then pointed to a chair. "Sit down, Arlo." Once Fetter was seated, the sheriff continued, "The stage has been attacked by Indians. Thomas claims it was Victorio, but I'm sure he doesn't have any idea who did it."

Fetter jerked forward in the chair, his knuckles turning white where he gripped the edge of the pine desk. "Did they get the Wells Fargo shipment?"

The sheriff tried moving his leg in the cast. "Danged leg. It itches like blazes, and I've still got another four more weeks in this thing. I shoulda shot that blamed horse."

Jack kept the smile from his face. He had heard the story of Sheriff Raymond Beasley's broken leg from Doc Pratt, and none of the blame could have rested on the horse. The sheriff was a prosperous-looking man, and his weight had increased significantly over the past few years, especially around the middle. He had attempted to swing into his saddle, and, just before reaching halfway, lost his balance and fell backward. His body twisted as he fell, and his thigh, midway between hip and knee, took all of his weight when he crashed into the rim of a bucket he had left outside instead of putting back in the barn. The doc said, fortunately, it only cracked his thigh bone. He still put the sheriff in a cast to keep him as immobile as possible. But the sheriff's horse was now taking the brunt of the blame.

Sheriff Beasley, still messing with his cast, said in a slightly peeved voice, "I don't know what was took, Arlo. I just heard about it myself."

Fetter, almost beside himself, removed a handkerchief from inside his coat, took off his bowler hat, and wiped his forehead and thinning brown hair. "Sheriff, the main office is going to go crazy if this shipment was taken. We had over eighty thousand dollars' worth of gold bullion on that stage." Fetter turned to look at Jack, who was leaning against the wall behind him. "While you were hunting Rush, we had a special gold shipment, with guards assigned, hijacked just outside of Las Cruces. That shipment was worth a hundred and twenty thousand dollars. That makes a total of two hundred thousand dollars we've shipped that has been stolen."

Beasley looked at Jack. "And four good men were killed."

Fetter nodded. "Yes, four men were killed. So what are you planning on doing? Do you think it's Indians like Mr. Chase claimed? Is Victorio taking the gold to provide his warriors guns and ammunition? How do you plan on getting the gold back?"

Leaving his leg be, the sheriff turned a haggard face toward Arlo Fetter. "Arlo, we'll investigate. I can't tell you whether it was Victorio or who it was, but we'll find out. That's all we can do."

Jack thought, *Stealing gold doesn't sound like any Indians I've had dealings with.* "Sheriff, when did the first robbery take place?"

The sheriff began pondering the question.

Fetter popped up. "October the eleventh would've been about right, figuring their departure date."

"Good. I was brought back around October the sixteenth. I saw Victorio four days earlier. In fact, according to the rancher who brought me in, Victorio was with the group that turned me over to him the day before I showed up here. He couldn't have been in two places at the same time. Look how far away Las Cruces is. Based on that, I'd say Victorio is cleared of the first theft. You've either got another tribe doing the massacres, or a bunch of white men masquerading as Indians."

Fetter had been staring at Jack. He spun around and faced Sheriff Beasley. "What about that, Sheriff? Could it be white men?"

Beasley nodded. "Sure it could, but it could be another tribe of Indians, too. We've got to investigate before we can go jumping to conclusions, especially far-fetched ones like it must be white men dressed up as Indians."

Fetter jumped to his feet. "Good, then let's go, let's investigate." He looked at Beasley's leg. "Can you ride with that thing?"

"Not a chance. In a couple of weeks, when this cast comes off, I'll ride out and take a look."

Jack straightened from the wall he had been leaning against. "Doc says you'll be in that cast at least four more weeks, Sheriff."

The sheriff stiffened. "Seems the doc tells you everything about his patients."

"Nope, just the good stuff."

The sheriff's face turned red, but Fetter didn't notice. "Four weeks. I can't wait that long to let the home office know what's going on."

Before the sheriff could answer, Jack spoke up. "Mr. Fetter, Indians don't usually mess with gold except for ornaments. What size bars did you ship?"

"Same size both times, four-hundred-troy-ounce bars. That's about twenty-seven pounds a bar. The first shipment . . . let me see."

The man began to figure in his head. He figured for a minute or so and stopped. "The wagon had fourteen bars. Each bar is roughly twenty-seven pounds and worth about eighty-six hundred dollars. The stage left with nine bars. Again, the same value for each bar, and their total weight would be 240 pounds, give or take a few pounds."

Jack looked at the sheriff. "Do you really think Victorio, who couldn't make it to where the first robbery took place because he was with me, would haul around something that weighed two hundred and forty pounds? Even if you do, it doesn't explain the first robbery."

The sheriff moved around in his chair. Using both hands, he lifted his leg from its chair rest and allowed his heel to sit on the floor. He let out a big sigh, pressed down on his chair's armrests, lifted himself, and slid as far back in his chair as he could. Then he cleared his throat. "Well, I wouldn't say you're right, because nobody can know what another man is thinking, but I'll give you the possibility that you *may* be right."

Fetter looked at Jack, then back at the sheriff, then returned to Jack. "So what do we do?"

Jack was tired of beating around the bush with this sheriff, who appeared to be lazy to the extreme. "Here's what I'd do. Two, maybe three men could ride out to the ambush site and examine it. The thieves, whether white or Indian, will be long gone, especially in this weather."

All the while Jack was talking, Fetter's head was nodding up and down. "Good. Let's be on our way."

Jack shook his head. "Hold on, Mr. Fetter. Whoever's going needs to get a couple of folks to go with him. They both need to be lawmen, good trackers, and good shots. So that'll take a bit."

"I want to go."

"I know you do, but you've seen the weather. The men who go out there need to be seasoned. They need to know what they're doing so that each man can depend on the other. As willing and anxious as you are to go, I'm sorry to tell you, you don't fit what's needed. You go back to your office. Whoever's heading this up will stop by before they leave and let you know their plans, but that's the best we can do."

Fetter took a deep breath. He bit his lower lip, released it, and spoke. "I'll be waiting in my office. Please make it soon." The man turned and marched from the sheriff's office. A cold blast of wind filled the room when he opened the door.

The sheriff motioned toward the coffeepot. "Whew, talk about a bucket of worms, and in this weather. Billy, could you get me a cup of coffee? We'll wait until this storm clears and it warms, and then ride out there. With this cold weather, everything'll be fine."

Jack couldn't believe what he was hearing. The sheriff was

going to leave those folks out at the ambush site until the storm cleared? Not in his lifetime. "I'm leaving as soon as I can. With this wind, the tracks will be gone, and if it warms up and starts raining, all the sign will be lost. I have a proposal for you."

Shocked, Sheriff Beasley stared at Jack.

14

"You're crazy."

Jack shook his head. "I'm not crazy. I have a job to do. You're laid up, but I need some help. How about I deputize Billy? He'll give me an additional man. He knows which end the lead comes out of, and right now, that's what I need."

Billy pushed away from the wall. "I'm not just a pretty face, Jack. I can track with the best of them."

Jack turned toward the younger man, his face reflecting surprise. "Good, another bonus." Turning back to the sheriff, he could see the man trying to come up with an objection. "Look, Sheriff. You can't make a move with your leg like it is. I don't expect you to. But you can contribute through Billy. That might help you when the next election comes along." He could see mentioning the election had gotten the man's attention.

The sheriff turned to Billy. "Is that alright with you, Billy? I wouldn't want you to have to go out in that weather if you didn't want to."

"Yes, sir. It's fine with me. I'm glad I can help, and we need to get those poor folks back, along with that gold if it's still there."

The sheriff, obviously not happy with the way things had

turned out, but resigned to the result, nodded. "Alright, but I have some things Billy needs to take care of today. He can't leave until tomorrow."

Jack was taken aback, but before he could say anything, Billy blurted out, "What kinds of things?"

Beasley fumbled in his desk, finally bringing out an official document. "The bank has an order of eviction." He held it up. "You need to serve this today, and it'll be necessary for you to lock up tonight. I can't do it with this bum leg."

Billy stepped forward and jerked the order of eviction from the sheriff's hand. He looked at it and tossed it back on the table. "You could serve that in a wagon."

The sheriff's voice took on a wheedling tone. "You know how hard it is for me to get into a wagon and then ride over a rough road with this leg. You need to do these kinda things until I'm back on my feet."

Billy jerked the badge from his chest and skidded it across the desk until it hit the sheriff's belly. "I quit. You figure out how to serve that eviction and lock up. Maybe the town drunk will be willing to help."

Jack, seeing the shocked look on the sheriff's face, almost burst out laughing. *Good for you, Billy*, he thought.

The younger man slapped his hat on his blond hair, grabbed his coat, and headed for the door. Over his shoulder he tossed to Jack, "You coming with me?"

Jack looked at the sheriff and shrugged his shoulders. "You bet. I'm right behind you." The door opened, and the northwest wind slammed them both in the face. Jack felt the warmth of the room on his back disappear as he pulled the door closed.

Billy spun around. "Guess I lost my temper."

Jack grinned. "I guess you did. Come on. Too late to change your mind now." He headed straight for Andy's gun shop. Reaching it, he swung the door open and stepped inside, Billy crowding in behind him.

Footsteps sounded from behind the curtain in the workshop. Andy called, "Who the blazes is out in this weather?" He pushed through the drapes on the door, and his eyebrows rose at the two of them. "The question still stands. It's too cold to be out today. What's going on?"

Jack explained everything, through Billy quitting as deputy sheriff.

Andy wiped a spot of oil from the counter. "I thought you liked that job. You told me you were making a career out of the law."

"I am, but maybe a different trail. Who knows, if we get these robberies solved, I just might run for sheriff in Grant County. Beasley's been getting lazier every day. Maybe the folks haven't seen it yet, what with me doing all the work. But with me gone? We'll see."

"I'll vote for you," Andy said. "Too bad the women can't vote, or you'd be a shoo-in."

"Alright, you two, I've got business here." The two younger men grew serious. "Andy, you offered to help. Does your offer still stand?"

"Like a rock, Jack."

"Then I need you as a deputy, right now. Can you do that?"

Andy thought for a minute. "It gets pretty slow this time of year, and this weather's just about shut down my business. I don't have anything keeping me here. Sure, I'm ready."

"Good, the two of you raise your right hands."

Both men turned toward Jack and raised their right hands.

"Do you swear to uphold the law of this country and support your government?"

Two answers, "Yep," and, "I sure do," greeted his question.

Jack pulled the two deputy marshal badges from his pocket and gave one to Billy and the other to Andy. He watched as they pinned them on. "Alright, you are now officially targets for every bad guy around. Billy, you know a little about that. Andy, you'll find out."

"I've been down that path before, Jack."

Jack nodded. "Good. You can tell me about it sometime, but for now, let me have another two boxes of .44 Henry." Jack paid for the ammunition. "Figure on being out in this weather for at least a couple of weeks, and meet me at Tiny's with your gear. I've got to make a stop at the Bucket of Blood, but as soon as I finish there, I'll head down to the stables."

"Sure thing," Billy said and left the shop.

"Any questions?" Jack asked Andy as he watched the man take a Winchester off the rack.

"Nope, I've heard all I need to know."

Jack pulled his hat down, turned, and opened the door. The wind was still blasting off the mountains, and the snow was getting heavier. The street and housetops had turned white. This would be a tough night. At least they shouldn't have to worry about Indians or outlaws. He figured they were all curled up in front of their fires. Out of habit he checked for traffic, but only an occasional ore wagon rolled down the street. He strode to the other side and opened the door to the Bucket of Blood saloon, stepped in, and looked around. A few diehard patrons were scattered around the tables. The weather had hurt business even here. Jack wanted to talk to Bramley, the owner. In his experience, saloon owners knew just about everything that was going on in the country. Miners, cowhands, and outlaws all frequented the saloons and had their stories to tell. They were the source of just about any information a man was looking for.

Jack walked to the bar. The wind outside was doing at least one good thing. Through cracks and holes in the wall, it was removing the smoke and stench of cigarettes, cigars, and unwashed spittoons. Jack surveyed the reflection of the crowd in the long mirror hanging above the shelf against the back wall. An assortment of colored bottles crowded along the shelf, waiting for someone to grab them by their long necks. Bramley, behind the bar, had seen Jack enter. He slowly made his way toward him.

"Want a drink, Marshal? It'll warm you up."

"Better a coffee. I'm about to head out, and it's gonna be a cold trip."

Bramley nodded. "One cup coming up." He looked at the woman working the other end of the bar and pantomimed drinking a cup of coffee. She nodded and slipped through the door to the kitchen. In moments she was back with a cup, a small pitcher of cream, and a jar of sugar, a spoon stabbed into the middle of the jar. She placed everything in front of Jack and moved back to her previous position, wiping spots of liquid from the bar's surface as she passed. Jack began spooning sugar into his steaming coffee. "Have you heard anything about Rush's crew?"

Bramley never moved. He was leaning against the back counter behind the bar. "Watch your back, Marshal. There's five of the Rush bunch in town, and they're spending money like they hit the mother lode. Three are here. Check in the back corner. You'll see two cowhands. The third fella is a gunfighter. He's all dressed in black. You probably can't see them from here, but I swear, he has the coldest blue eyes I've ever seen. He just looks at you and you get a chill. They're on the prod, so be ready. I've got my greener if you need help. Maybe it won't come to that."

Jack unbuttoned his two coats, made sure the right side was back, freeing one of his Smith and Wessons. In the mirror, he recognized the gunfighter. He was the one who had calmly watched while Jack was hanged. He could feel the cold rage begin to build. *I need to get on down the road,* he thought, *but I've got time for you.* He took another sip of the coffee. It wasn't the best, but it was certainly better than trail coffee, and the sugar and cream dulled the bite.

He continued to watch the table with the three Triple Six hands. They hadn't recognized him yet, and that was well and good. He wanted to give them a big surprise. Maybe make them a little jumpy. He took another sip of coffee, placed the cup on the bar, and turned around. In a loud, harsh voice he called to the back table, "You boys hanged anyone lately? You weren't too successful with me."

He saw the shock on the men's faces. They weren't mentally prepared for a confrontation now. They had come into town to party, have fun, and here they were being called out by a man they knew was dead. "You're looking a little shocked there, blue-eyes. Maybe I can help you. You sat back all nice and relaxed while that crazy kid and his old man stretched my neck. Is that clearing things up a mite for you?" Jack moved his coattails behind his left revolver. Now both weapons were like him, ready. He was feeling good. He hadn't felt this good in a while.

Come on, boys, he thought, *make it happen*. He stepped away from the bar, taking one step, and stopped. He realized he was smiling. Jack knew how unnerving such a tactic could be. Today, it would work for him. His smile grew. "Having a tough time recognizing me, boys?" He reached up with his left hand and ripped his bandanna from around his neck, exposing the proud flesh. The scabs were gone, but the skin was bright red, gathered in places, no longer smooth like the rest of his neck.

Yanking the bandanna from his neck brought audible gasps from the other patrons. Several jumped from their chairs and rapidly made their way to and out the door. The others between him and the gunman jumped from their seats, either moving to the wall and standing or to tables as far out of the way as possible. Experienced westerners knew that a gunfight in a saloon could end up getting more people shot than just the combatants.

The gunfighter, dressed in black, leaned his chair onto its back legs. "Well, I'll be, and here I thought Rush had killed you for sure. How'd you survive that fall? It was a long ways down to those rocks, and I saw several of the boys taking potshots at you." He sneered. "Not me, I kill a man standing up, facing me."

Jack's smile grew wider. "Looks like you've got your chance, today." Jack looked at the other two men. "You boys in this? If you are, it's no problem for me. I just don't want to kill an innocent person who might've made too quick a move. You know, making me think he's going for his gun."

The one on the side nearest the wall raised his hands and slowly stood, easing away from the table. "I ain't interested in this fight a-tall, Mr. Marshal, not a-tall."

"Then you move to the wall and shuck your weapon with your thumb and forefinger. Do it slowly." Jack raised his voice. "Bramley, could you cover this fine fella with your greener?"

"I'd be glad to, Jack."

At the mention of the shotgun, the man on the opposite side of the table looked at the gunfighter. "Pax, I ain't got a quarrel with this here marshal. I hope you understand. I'm stepping out."

The man stood, his hands high.

Jack motioned with his head. "Move over with your friend and shuck that shooter the same way. You got an eye on 'em, Bramley?"

"I do, Marshal. You don't need to worry a bit about these two fellers. You boys come on over here."

Jack smiled at Pax. "Looks like it's the way you like it, pardner. Just you and me. You want to stand up, drop your gun, and I'll take you to jail, or is this your day for mistakes? By the way, what's your name? I heard that fella call you Pax."

The gunfighter pushed his chair back from the table. The legs screeched across the rough-cut floor of the saloon. When he was well clear, he stood and returned Jack's smile. "The name is Paxton Garfield, but a lot of folks call me Pax or Black Pax. I can make the day pretty black for most people."

"I bet you can, Mr. Black Pax. Now how about you do like your compadres and shuck those shooters."

"It's a cold day out there, Marshal. You wouldn't think the rats would desert you when it's so warm in here, but they still do."

Jack nodded. "The only ones you can depend on are family and friends. I've never seen a dependable gunman."

"Oh, I have to disagree, Marshal. I'm dependable. I do what I say, and I say I'm going to kill you. I like you, especially what I saw of you at the hanging tree, but you see, Marshal, you're on the wrong side, and I've already taken the man's money."

The saloon had become deathly quiet. The only sound was the wind and a loose shutter banging against a window. There was no talking, no tinkling glasses, no laughing, only the wind and the bang of the shutter.

"I'm mighty sorry I've got to kill you, Marshal, but when that shutter bangs again, I'm drawing."

Jack gave a slow nod. "When the shutter bangs, Pax."

Jack, especially over the last week, as he started feeling better, had been getting out to the foothills and practicing with his new Smith and Wesson Americans. He wasn't positive, but he actually felt faster with them than he had with the Remingtons. *I guess this is the test,* he thought and listened.

There was a lull in the wind. It was so quiet in the saloon, Jack could hear heavy breathing from one of the patrons. A mouse scurried across the floor. But the quiet didn't last. The wind picked up. Moments later it was howling.

The shutter banged.

Jack watched Black Pax Garfield's right hand flash to his Colt. *He is quick,* Jack thought, but knew he had the man beat, and he could see Garfield knew it too, but he was game.

The gunfighter's Colt was clearing the holster, and the muzzle began to swing up when Jack fired the first shot from the Smith and Wesson .44. It bucked in his hand, and the heavy two-hundred-grain bullet plowed into Garfield's chest. A red spot, harder to see than normal in the black cloth, appeared on the man's shirt. He staggered back. He hadn't fired when he was hit. Jack admired Garfield's control. The Colt had lowered a bit, but was starting back up again. The gunfighter's blue eyes were locked on Jack's.

Jack shook his head, telling the man not to do it, but the Colt's muzzle kept rising. Jack fired again, putting the bullet within an inch of the first one. Garfield staggered farther back against a table, which gave him support. The effort of lifting the Colt was etched on his face, but so was determination. The Colt lifted for the third time. Jack fired his last shot, the bullet striking the gunfighter between and just above his eyebrows. He folded like a puppet whose strings had been cut, crumpling to the floor.

Jack called to Bramley, "Have someone go get the undertaker."

"Sure he don't need the doc?"

"He won't ever be needing a doctor again."

Bramley sent one of the patrons, with the promise of a free drink, after the undertaker. Carrying his shotgun, he ambled over to Jack and looked down at Garfield.

"You'll be collecting a bounty on him. I've seen that name on a wanted poster somewhere." He shook his head. "That feller had sand."

"Yeah, too bad he didn't direct it for good."

Bramley shook his head. "It's funny the people who head out west. We get all kinds."

The door opened and closed. Jack expected the undertaker, but Andy stepped up.

"You've been busy."

"Wasn't my intent." He nodded toward Bramley. "He saved my bacon. I had no idea they were here. Funny thing, though, I don't think Garfield would have ambushed me. Those other two might have, if they'd recognized me, but not him." Jack shook his head again. "You can never tell about people."

Andy walked over and looked at Garfield, then looked back at Jack. "In the head?"

"I had to stop him before an innocent person got hit by a stray bullet. He wouldn't quit. He took the first two in the heart, and each time he kept bringing up his pistol."

Andy picked up Garfield's Colt. He looked at it, then smelled the weapon. "He never fired?"

Jack nodded. "That's the funny thing. You know how a man tends to fire when he's hit, just from the shock of the bullet?"

Andy nodded.

"He didn't. He maintained control throughout. Every time a slug hit him, his weapon lowered, and then he'd bring it back up. He always had it under control, hoping to get me lined up, but he never did, so he never fired."

The three men stared down at the dead man. Jack wondered how many lives Garfield had taken. What had propelled him down his ill-fated path? Where had he come from, a poor family or a rich one, happy or joyless? He remembered the cold eyes. *It was probably the war,* he thought. *So much killing changes people. I know it's changed me, but at least I've stayed on the right side.* His mind was quiet for a moment, then, *At least I hope so.*

The undertaker showed up with help, and they carted the body into the cold, blustery day. Jack stepped back up to his coffee and took a sip. It was still hot.

Andy, at his elbow, leaned on the bar toward him.

Jack motioned his head toward the prisoners. "Why don't you take these two down to the sheriff and tell him to hold them until we get back. Mr. Bramley said there were two more in town. We need to look for them before we take off."

Andy shook his head. "No need. I saw two riders mount and tear out of here like scalded dogs just before the shooting started. Pretty sure it was them. Somebody got word to 'em."

Jack nodded. "Probably right. In that case, drop these off, and I'll see you at Tiny's as soon as I finish my coffee."

"Right, boss."

Andy herded the two Rush men through the door, and Jack took another sip of coffee.

15

Billy blew into his gloved hands. "Whew, I don't think I've been this cold since I was working on a mining crew up in Colorado. Figured I'd be turning into an icicle afore I got out of there."

The three men had pulled up on a rise, looking down on the blackened hulk of the stagecoach and the remains of the bodies. Jack, riding between the two other men, shook his head and muttered something under his breath.

Billy, on his right side, looked at him. "What was that, Jack?"

"Just talking to myself. I said it wouldn't have happened if the stage hadn't included that gold. Those folks would still be alive. That's the thing about Butterfield's operation. They don't allow valuables. That's why they haven't been robbed. Those folks got murdered for a pile of yellow metal."

He bumped Smokey in the flanks. "Let's go on down and see if we can find out anything. Stay together. I don't want to destroy any more sign than we have to, and keep your eyes open. I don't expect trouble, but you can't be too careful." He flipped the loops holding the six-guns in place from each of the Smiths' hammers, and checked the Winchester was loose in the scabbard. He was gratified to find his two deputies did the same thing. Both were ready.

Jack nodded at a lone stand of sagebrush about thirty yards from the coach. "We'll tie up there and walk in."

The three pulled up at the sagebrush and dismounted. Stonewall moved up to the side of Smokey. The mule stood so close Jack could barely remove his right boot from the stirrup. He patted Smokey on the neck before dismounting, reached over and gave Stonewall a couple of pats, even though he was irritated at the mule for sidling in so close to Smokey. He squeezed his foot out of the stirrup, pulled his leg from between the two animals, and dismounted.

Andy and Billy were already down and watching him. Billy was the first to speak. "That mule must like you a lot. He got in a little tight."

Jack grunted. "It's not me that danged hardhead likes so much, it's Smokey. They've been together quite a few years."

"Well, I noticed when you tried to get down, he turned his head and was nuzzling you. Tells me he likes you."

"He likes these." Jack pulled one of the animals' cookies from his pocket. He broke it in thirds, took a piece and handed one to each of the men.

Andy looked at the cookie, smelled it, took a small bite, and chewed for a minute. "That's mighty good, Jack."

"The mule and horses think so, too."

"Where'd you get 'em? Does Tiny make them?"

"Nope, well, he may now. I gave him the recipe. But I got the original recipe from the rancher in Texas where I bought Thunder and Pepper. He said his ranch hands liked them about as much as the animals did."

Billy hesitantly took a bite. He chewed for a moment, then shoved the remainder into his mouth. With his mouth full, he said, "Mighty good," and in the process, spit a hunk of oatmeal on Jack's coat.

Jack nodded, wiped it off, and watching the ground closely, walked to the stagecoach. His mind was working on the loading problem for the coach. The driver wouldn't have wanted all of the weight on the front axle or the back. He would have split the weight, so his bet was there would have been two strongboxes, each weighing a little over a hundred pounds. He'd also bet they wouldn't be here. That was the reason this stage had been hit. The sheriff seemed convinced it was an Indian raid, but Jack was equally convinced the sheriff didn't know what he was talking about.

One body, half in and half out of the coach, was burned beyond any chance of recognition. It looked like this was probably one of the men. He was lucky. By all indications he'd been killed by a bullet. The blackened metal of his six-gun was still gripped in his charred hand. *The people who did this,* Jack thought, *were brutal. They'd better hope I don't find them. There are a few people who might say I can be pretty brutal myself.*

As expected, Jack found no sign of the strongboxes. There was nothing that indicated there was one box or two that had been carried on the coach. The coach itself had become a frail, black skeleton, leaving nothing to hint of the men who did this awful act.

Andy called softly from among several stands of sage, "Jack, I found the lady."

"Any sign around her?"

"Plenty."

Jack took a deep breath. He didn't like the ominous sound of Andy's voice and was sure he didn't want to see what the deputy had found. He stepped carefully so as not to blur any sign or tracks. Nearing where Andy stood, Jack saw a bare foot and part of a leg extending from behind the sagebrush. He turned to Billy, who was searching on the other side of the coach. "Billy, have you seen any blankets?"

"Yeah, Jack. There's one over here. Looks like the one Blaine Oats, the driver, always wore over his legs when it was chilly."

"Would you bring it? We're gonna need something to cover up this lady."

"Sure." Moments later Billy was at Jack's side. He handed him the blanket.

"Thanks. You can go on and continue the search."

His voice somber, Billy said, "No, Jack. Reckon I oughta see what these vermin are capable of."

"You ever been involved in anything like this?"

The big blond man shook his head. "No. I've dealt with a few shootings. I once had to help the sheriff investigate a case where a sodbuster went crazy and killed his whole family, even the little kids, but I've never dealt with a lady being treated like this."

Jack nodded and stepped forward. She looked to be in her early fifties. Her dress had been ripped from her body, along with her undergarments. Jack covered her with the blanket. The woman's face was anything but serene. From what could be seen, she looked like she had died in terrible agony. Before he covered her, he inspected the ugly, ripping knife wound in her belly. Her face was beaten beyond recognition. The cuts and bruises had turned black. He had seen more than he wanted to see. He pulled the blanket over the woman's face and heard someone retching.

Turning, Jack saw Billy leaning against the burned stage-coach, throwing up. It looked and sounded as if he were emptying his entire body. He looked at Andy, who had been standing next to the lady, staring at her face.

Andy returned the look. "You've seen this before?"

"Wars," Jack said, "seems like they give some men permission to turn into animals, while others rise to be heroes."

"Me too. I was hoping I'd never see anything like it again."

Jack nodded. "Sorry you had to. You can go home anytime you feel the need, and there'll be no hard feelings."

"Wasn't sayin' that, Jack. I just don't like what I'm looking at. It makes me want to get somebody in my sights, close or far, makes no difference."

Jack continued to look down at the covered body. A few curls of her gray hair escaped from under the blanket's edge. Finally, he shook his head and began to examine the ground around her. He found no tracks other than the moccasin prints. For most people that would be enough to satisfy them it was Indians, but he didn't really think Indians had anything to do with this massacre. Jack kept searching around her. He came back to the moccasin prints. One of them was only half visible, like it had been stepped on, but there wasn't a print over it.

He kneeled on the sandy ground, getting his eyes within inches of the sand and dirt granules, and then he saw it. It wasn't a boot or moccasin print, but just a soft indentation over the toe of the moccasin. He searched for similar markings and found more. Jack sat back on his heels and thought about what could have made these dents. An idea struck him. He sat back, lifted his leg, grabbed his boot, and twisted his foot so he could look at the sole. *That's it,* he thought. *That's how they did it.*

"Andy, how many riders do you figure were here based on the sign?"

The gunsmith deputy had moved out about thirty yards while he circled the final resting place of the stage and its occupants. "From what the tracks are telling me, there were only three unshod horses. Those three rode around a lot. You can also see where the same moccasined feet went back and forth. It's like they were trying to appear to be more people, but it's pretty easy to read the distinct tracks, and I'll swear it was the same three."

"Do you believe three could have done all this?"

Andy shook his head. "No way. This was the job of at least six, maybe more. Three people could never have gotten Blaine to stop." Andy shoved his hat to the back of his head and scratched his forehead in consternation. "But I can't find the sign of any more than three people."

Jack looked at the indentation again. "I have, and it reminds me of a case I had back in Texas. There was an outfit that covered their horses' hooves with hides, leaving only a faint impression in the ground. Start looking for impressions, not hooves. I guarantee that's what this bunch is doing."

Only minutes passed before Andy spoke up. "Here it is. I see what you're talking about. I found dents blocking parts of unshod tracks. That's pretty slick."

"Slick or not, we're onto them. Keep looking." Jack moved out from the woman's body and, now that he knew what he was looking for, found a clear set of impressions. He continued looking and found more sign.

Billy spoke up from behind a patch of large red boulders off to the side of the road. "I found a spot where two horses were standing behind these boulders. I think you've nailed it, Jack. These weren't Indians. I'm betting they were white men. They only just pretended to be Indians to throw us off the track."

Jack shot an index finger toward Billy when he stepped out from behind the mass of boulders. "Good catch, Billy. Yep, if we had blamed the Indians, whoever did this would have been free and clear, nothing to worry about. But we've seen their cards now. Let's get these folks buried. If you can find anything identifying them, take it, plus whatever valuables the killers missed. Their kin will be glad to get whatever we can find."

Jack had included two shovels on Stonewall's pack. He untied the shovels and then removed each of the packs, lifting them from Stonewall's back to give him a little respite. The mule turned his head to watch, reached his long neck, and bumped Jack on the shoulder. He started to smell around Jack's coat.

"You'd better give that mule one of them cookies afore he takes a bite out of you," Billy called. The three men laughed, the sound disappearing quickly across the sagebrush plains. *Funny,* Jack thought, *how the human mind can become used to such horrible occurrences. Maybe humor is a protection.* He unconsciously shrugged the thought away. Before leaving Stonewall and the horses, he gave each one half of a cookie. Contented, they munched their treat.

With the two shovels in hand, he headed for a clear spot that was large enough to hold the graves. "Andy, keep watch. Billy and I will start digging. We'll switch off, but I want to keep one person watching at all times. I don't expect anyone, but I'd hate for Victorio or any of his men to surprise us."

Billy picked up one of the shovels and drove the blade deep into the earth, lifting out the first shovel of dirt. Jack followed suit. There was no talking, only the quiet of the plains and the swish of the shovels driving into the ground. An occasional desert wren lent her music to the rhythmic sound of shovels and dirt. Buzzards circled patiently high above in the deep blue sky, unaware this would be one meal they would miss.

Jack shed his long coat, and before much time passed, he pulled off his jacket. The wind had died, and though it was still cold, there was a cloudless, blue sky. The sun gradually warmed the desert and the working men.

An hour passed. Billy had removed his coat and laid his hat on top. His blond hair glistened in the sun. Watching the open plains to ensure there were no surprises, Andy glanced at his friend, the sun glinting off his golden hair. He gave a long, low whistle. "Billy, could you put your hat back on. That hair will show up twenty miles away. If Victorio sees it, he'll be wanting to give it to his new bride."

Sweat had begun popping out on the blond deputy's face. He stopped, removed his bandanna and wiped his forehead. When he was done, he retied the bandanna around his neck and gazed across the jagged plains. "Andy, you'd best be nice to me. Victorio and I are mighty good friends. He admires my golden locks, yes, sir, he surely does. If he shows up, I might just be your ticket to safety." He moved the shovel to between his knees and, using both hands, smoothed his hair back.

Jack threw another shovel of dirt on the pile and glanced at the two men. "Why don't you lovebirds switch places. I'd like to get this finished today."

"Sure thing, boss," Andy called, and swung down from his horse. He led it to where the others were tied, untied Billy's, and brought his back with him. They switched places, and the digging continued.

Shortly after noon, Jack stopped and looked at the holes. "I think that'll do. We'll bury them and pile some rocks on top. That should be plenty of protection. Let's get the bodies."

The last to be laid in her grave was the lady. They had wrapped her in the blanket and gently placed her in the lonely hole. Andy and Billy looked at Jack. Andy spoke up. "You gonna say some words over them, boss?"

Jack nodded. "Sure." With his left hand he grasped the crown of his gray Stetson, lifted it from his head, and placed it over his heart. "Lord, these fine folks met a tragic end here in this New Mexico desert. I don't know anything about them except they were yours, and they were murdered most viciously. We'd appreciate it if you could let their bodies lie here nice and peaceable. Don't worry about those fellas who did this. We'll take care of them. Amen." Jack settled his Stetson back on his head, walked to his coats, and slipped them on. "You boys cover them up good. I'm gonna have a look farther out to see if I can find where they shucked those skins."

Jack, without waiting for acknowledgment, stepped to Smokey and swung into the saddle. He turned the grulla back the way they had come. When he had ridden a couple of hundred yards, he began the circle around the ambush. He kept the burned-out stage on his left and maintained a constant distance. Jack rode slow and steady, checking the ground. The sound of Smokey's hoofbeats were like syncopation to the rhythmic swish of the shovels. He had circled almost one hundred and eighty degrees when he saw the tracks. Those of the unshod ponies were clear, leading away and to the southeast. The only things in that direction, besides the Organ Mountains, were Mesilla, Las Cruces, and El Paso.

He turned in the saddle to check on the deputies' progress. They were carrying rocks. Andy placed a large rock on a grave and waved him back. He put Smokey into a lope and was back at the gravesites in no time.

"We're done."

"Good, let me get the packs on Stonewall, and we'll be on our way." He walked Smokey to Stonewall, and while the horse and mule pulled at bunch grass, he loaded the mule's packs and tied them down. Billy brought the shovels, and Jack secured them.

Andy called from the gravesite, "You two about ready to ride?"

"Just about." He finished the last knot and walked to the grulla. Swinging into the saddle, he glanced back to see Andy pointing toward the northwest. There was a slow-moving dust cloud approaching. He motioned to Billy, who had mounted and was leading Andy's horse. The two of them, with Jack leading Stonewall, made their way back to Andy and the graves.

Jack leaned forward on the saddle horn. "What do you think?"

Andy shrugged. "Could be 'Paches, but I'm thinkin' not. They're coming awful slow. More like travelers, probably a wagon or buckboard."

Andy mounted, and the three men watched the approaching dust cloud. Soon it was close enough to see the buckboard drawn by two horses and occupied by two men.

16

The buckboard, containing Arlo Fetter, the Wells Fargo agent in Silver City, and United States Marshal Quint Hardwick, rolled to a stop. Hardwick turned cold eyes toward Jack. "What the blue blazes are you doing out here chasing Indians? I gave you orders to capture Elijah Rush and his gang, not dawdle after a bunch of Apaches."

Jack stared at the lawman. Seconds ticked by.

Hardwick frowned. "Did you hear me?"

Jack held the man's stare and responded in a low gravelly voice, "Are you done?"

Jack watched the ends of Hardwick's perfectly curled mustache move with the clinching of his jaws. He finally decided. "Yes."

"Good. There's something I don't think you've gotten through that hard head of yours. I don't work for you. I was appointed by Judge Coleman, and I work directly for him. I owe you no explanation of how I act or who I pursue. Am I being clear enough for you? Furthermore, what are you doing out here in a buckboard? If it was Apaches, they'd already have you stretched out over a fire or a bed of red ants."

Hardwick's cheeks and forehead turned red. Few people talked to him the way Jack had just spoken, and most of those were dead or in prison. His pupils, already small in the bright light, shrank even smaller. His eyes tightened. "I've killed men who've talked to me like that, Sage, but I've never killed a man with a badge. You listen to me and listen good. You may be hired by Judge Coleman, but you'll follow my orders. I can send a telegram to Washington and have your badge anytime I want. Make sure *you* understand that."

Jack removed the badge and hefted it in his left hand. "Marshal, I didn't want this badge to begin with, and if you want it, you can have it right now. I've got other work I'd rather be doing." He held it out to Hardwick.

The marshal studied the badge closely, as if he was actually considering taking it. Finally he shook his head, and his voice dropped to a friendlier tone. "You keep it. Judge Coleman did appoint you, but you need to be chasing Rush, not Indians."

Jack leaned forward. "That's what I've been trying to tell you. This stage was robbed by white men trying to make out like they were Indians. They were after the gold." Jack shot an accusing look at Fetter, but didn't pursue it.

Fetter looked away and said nothing.

Hardwick's curiosity overrode his anger. "How do you know?"

Jack swung down from Smokey. "Over here." He motioned for Hardwick to join him. Fetter wrapped the reins around the brake handle and stepped down, following the marshal.

Jack started to stop the man, but he was the Wells Fargo agent. Maybe his report would stop the shipment of valuables with passenger-carrying stages. If the decision wasn't made to change their policy, more people would die, not just here, but across the west.

Approaching the telltale horse tracks, Jack held out his arm. "Watch where you step. This is one of the places where we found definite sign." He knelt next to a print of an unshod hoof. It was partially obliterated by a blur. "Notice how this track is blocked out, but there's no obvious track erasing the hoofprint. Everything is clear until the edges just disappear around the front of the hoof, then clear on both sides. What could have caused that?"

Fetter straightened and rubbed his chin, his face scrunched in consternation, but Hardwick immediately came to the correct conclusion. He leaned over and pointed to the obliterated portion of the track.

"See where it's blanked out? There's a fuzzy outline around it." His finger moved closer to the track. "There, you can see a vague indentation. You're looking at a hoof that's got something wrapped around it." He stood where he was and looked around the immediate area, pointing again. "There, more tracks. A good tracker could follow those tracks, but he'd have to take it slow. They're mighty faint."

He turned to Jack, nodding. "White men for sure. Injuns have no call to hide their tracks. In fact, these are unshod horses. Someone's trying to put the blame on the Apaches and get off with a pile of gold. You have any idea who?"

Jack nodded. "I do. I think it's Elijah Rush and his bunch."

Fetter was the first to reply. "Rush? Marshal, do you know how far Rush's ranch is from here? This ambush was done way to the southeast of Silver City, and Rush has his place in about the roughest country you can find, way into the mountains west of town. You think he'd ride that far and take a big chance of running into Apaches or having the army cross his trail?"

"How much did you say Wells Fargo has lost in the past month?"

Fetter paused for a second, then quietly stated, "Over two hundred thousand dollars."

"Doesn't that answer your own question?"

Fetter said nothing.

Ignoring the Wells Fargo agent, Marshal Hardwick asked, "Have you found their tracks leaving here?"

"We have, and it's just a matter of time until they uncover their horses' hooves. They won't ride far with the hooves wrapped like that. If they were jumped by Apaches, they'd be in a world of trouble. They'd never outrun them."

"Are they going toward the Rush ranch?"

Jack pointed to the southeast. "No, they're headed off to the southeast. Roughly the same direction the stage was headed in, and they haven't turned yet. It's possible they could have a plan for getting rid of the gold. The border isn't far. Across the border, El Paso del Norte is large enough to give them an opportunity to do something with all that weight."

Hardwick frowned. "You don't think they'd swap gold for pesos, do you?"

Jack shook his head. "Definitely not, but they could take greenbacks. They're lighter and travel better. As soon as we leave, we'll be on their trail. They've got almost a three-day head start on us, but I think we'll catch up with them pretty quick. This is the second time they've hit the stage, and I imagine they're feeling pretty smug about now. No, I don't think they'll be suspecting anyone is after them."

Hardwick's face grew dark. "She was a schoolmarm."

Billy's head jerked around. "That wasn't Mrs. Graves?"

Hardwick nodded. "That's her. Madeline Graves. Everyone called her Mrs. Graves or Miss Maddy. Mighty nice lady. Came out a couple of years ago from the east to teach school in Silver City. She always said adventure wasn't only for the young. She wanted to see the wild west."

Billy stared at the woman's grave. "They beat her up so bad, I couldn't even recognize her." His normally laughing eyes were cold when he turned to Jack. "How can people do such awful things?"

Jack put a hand on the younger man's shoulder. "There's some bad folks in this world, Billy. In your job, you've seen some of them. Fortunately, there's not a lot of the type who do things like they did to Mrs. Graves. We're here to make sure they don't do it to anyone else." He gave the boy's shoulder a squeeze, released it, and turned to Hardwick. "We'll trail this bunch, but my bet is they'll stop in Mesilla, Las Cruces, or El Paso, maybe all three. The gold will be burning holes in their pockets. My bet is we'll catch them before the next three days are out."

Hardwick's pale gray eyes locked on Jack. "The judge likes crooks brought back for trial, but betwixt you and me, over their saddles, for this bunch, works just as well." He motioned to Fetter. "Let's go. We got no more business here."

Fetter looked at Jack. "Wells Fargo wants the gold back. There's a three percent reward for return of all or any portion of the gold."

Andy whistled.

Jack motioned to Andy and Billy. "Let's go." He started for Smokey, stopped, and turned to Fetter. "We'll get your gold, Arlo, but our first job is to catch those killers."

THE THREE MEN crossed the Rio Bravo just above Mesilla. They paused to allow the horses to drink. Streaks of orange and pink coursed across the scattered clouds. In the darkening blue sky, the sun was dipping lower in the west.

While the horses drank, Jack looked at the twinkling lights of the two towns, Mesilla and Las Cruces, separated by the Rio Bravo. The nearest was Mesilla, much larger and almost twice the size of its counterpart. "You boys know this country better than I do. Which one do you think they might have headed for, Mesilla or Las Cruces?"

Andy slid his hat to the back of his head. "My guess is Mesilla. I've always had more fun there. I personally find the women happier and less demanding. What do you think, Billy?"

The younger of the three nodded his head in agreement. "Mesilla. Food's better, if you like it spicy-hot."

Jack bumped Smokey. "Mesilla it is. Lead on, Andy, but be ready. We want to surprise them, not be surprised ourselves." The three men loosed their revolvers, trotting their horses toward the sound of singing, guitars, violins, and trumpets.

They pulled up to the first cantina, and Billy slid to the ground. He paused and stretched his back. "Umm, that feels good." Straightening, he looked up at Jack and Andy, both still mounted. Speaking louder because of the laughter and music, Billy said, "I know the bartender. I'll check and see if they've been here." As he was disappearing into the cantina, a man wearing a badge crossed the street toward them.

Andy leaned near Jack. "That's the town marshal, Lester Nelson. He's not a bad sort. Keeps a fairly clean town."

Jack appraised the man as he neared. He was of average height, maybe five feet seven or eight inches, dark hair, as best he could tell in the fading light. He wore his gun high on his right side.

"Evening, fellers, passing through?" Drawing closer, Lester recognized Andy. "Why howdy, Andy. Ain't seen you for a spell." He squinted at Andy's chest. "Is that a badge I see you wearing there?"

"It is, Lester, been deputized as a deputy U.S. Marshal." He nodded toward Jack. "Aim to give this here feller a hand."

Lester's eyes swung back to Jack. "You'd be?"

"Jack Sage."

"You the feller who rescued them little girls down El Paso way?"

"I am, Marshal, and we need your help. We're following at least six men. They robbed the Silver City stage and killed everyone aboard, including Mrs. Madeline Graves."

The town marshal's eyes narrowed. "Wasn't she the school-marm in Silver City?"

"That was her, and the outlaws were mighty brutal. They also stole a passel of gold."

The marshal nodded slowly. "They were here. Seven tough-looking hombres. Came in yesterday. One of them has him a girl-friend in El Paso. Her name's Rosita. My deputy heard him talking about her earlier today. Reckon that's why they pulled out. They did a lot of drinkin'. They were loud and threw their money around, but didn't cause any trouble."

Stonewall shook his head, pulling on the lead Jack held. "Easy does it, boy. We'll get that load off you in just a few minutes." He turned back to Lester. "When did they leave?"

"I'm thinking about an hour ago. Maybe two. Yeah, more like two. Like I said, this one feller was raring to get on to El Paso to see his girl."

"Marshal," Jack said, "did you hear any names?"

Marshal Nelson rubbed the stubble on his chin. "I did. Let me think." He stared along the street toward the Organ Mountains. Finally, his face lit with memory. "It was Ted. Yes, sir, Ted's the name. He's the one with the Rosita girl waiting for him." He nodded as he thought. "Yeah, and he looks to have a short fuse. He got right up in the face of several of his bunch. They all backed down quick-like."

Andy turned to Jack. "Could be one of the Rush boys. He's supposedly the oldest of the bunch, here, that is. Name is Theodore Rush, but he goes by Ted. Several of those boys have brought their guns by to be worked on. They don't mind talking. I heard another brother mentioned, an older one." Andy paused for a moment. "Emmett, that's his name. Seems he stayed in Texas when the family moved out here."

Billy walked out of the cantina and spotted the marshal. "Lester, you old son of a gun. How are you?" He gave the man a quick handshake.

"Doin' fine, Billy. Looks like you signed up with the govern-ment, too. You git tired of doing the sheriff's work for him?"

"Yep. I sure did."

"Thanks, Marshal," Jack said. "We'll be staying here tonight and heading out in the morning, early." He turned to Andy. "Where's a good place to stay?"

There was no hesitation. "Melana's Boarding House. Clean beds and the greatest food that's passed yore gums."

Marshal Nelson's head bobbed emphatically. "Yessiree, Bob. Best cookin' in town. I get by there almost every morning for breakfast."

Billy's head was going up and down in agreement as he swung into the saddle.

"Then Melana's it is. Take us to the best livery, Andy, and you can leave your horse. We'll take care of it while you make sure she has rooms for us." Jack touched his hat to the marshal. "Adios." He bumped Smokey, and they were off.

On the way to the stable, Billy asked, "Why don't we take out after 'em now? They're close."

"No. They're on rested horses. I want our animals to get a good rest before we leave here. It's going to be a dark night. My bet is they'll be stopping on the way, and I don't expect them to hurry. In fact, I expect them to be drinking when we get to El Paso. Give them enough time and the liquor will slow their gun hands and mess with their aim. I don't know if you've noticed, but we're a little outnumbered. If they're stupid enough to draw on us, it'll give us an edge."

Andy looked across at Billy and winked. "Smart."

17

The three marshals pulled up on a low ridgeline, something Jack would normally never do, but they were close to El Paso. The town's twinkling lights were visible in the darkening sky, and sounds of revelry drifted over the desert to meet them. Ted Rush had an itch to see a girl, and it was Jack's bet that he'd want to scratch that itch before they moved south of the river.

The two border towns were connected by a bridge built by the Spanish at Oñate Crossing. The crossing, even before the bridge had been built, lay along the Camino Real and offered the firmest footing for animals or men.

Jack marveled at the richness of the country along this portion of the Rio Bravo. Orchards of apple, peach, pear, and apricot lined the river for miles. The orchards were separated by acres of farmland growing wheat, corn, and melons. Farms lined both sides of the river. Small irrigation channels, acequias, gurgled while gently flowing through the towns. When he had passed through El Paso the last time, he had sampled some of the grapes and grape juice from the many vineyards. It was said the wine from El Paso del Norte rivaled the best of the continent.

Though El Paso was much smaller than its sister city across the Rio Bravo, its saloons were just as loud and rowdy. Passing the third one, they turned toward a narrow door sporting a sign over the entry proclaiming "Marshal's Office."

Jack looped Smokey's reins around the hitching rail and, with Andy and Billy behind him, walked into the office.

The marshal was sitting behind his desk, going through a stack of wanted circulars. At the sound of the men he looked up. His dark brown eyes, black in the lamplight, dropped to the badge on Jack's chest.

A grin split his sun-wrinkled face, separating his thick black mustache and even thicker goatee with a line of tobacco-stained teeth. "Well, I'll be. The last time I saw you, you were a Texas Ranger." He stood, stepped around the desk, and extended his scarred hand. "Now you're a deputy U.S. Marshal? I've gotta say, *Marshal* Sage, you get around." He looked at Andy and Billy and nodded. "Reckon these fellers are with you?"

Jack took the browned hand, enveloping it in his, and returned the man's grin. "Good to see you." He introduced Marshal Andrew McClintock and Marshal Bill Brice and shook his head. "That's a lot of marshals. How about if we call each other by first names. That might make it simpler."

He pointed at Andy and Billy, giving the marshal their names. "Call me Jack, and I don't think we were more than on nodding acquaintance the last time I was here, so I don't know yours."

Marshal Ruff returned to his chair, sat, and pointed at several chairs against the wall. "Seth is what my folks named me. Grab a chair and take a load off. What can I do for you?"

Jack and the deputies pulled chairs from the wall and placed them close to the desk. "Seth, we're looking for seven men. They robbed the Silver City stage and killed everyone on board, including a woman." Jack watched Seth Ruff's face harden. The man's eyes narrowed, and his lips drew into a thin line.

"You think they're here?"

Jack nodded. "Tracks were headed toward town, but with all the traffic on the road, we finally lost them. One thing we know for sure, though, they never left the road. They came into town. It's possible they may have crossed the river, but with all that gold, I'd suspect they'd stop to celebrate the first chance they had."

"Just the three of you after seven? This is my town. I'd like to help, and I have a good deputy. He's taking a stroll down main street right now, but he'll be back any minute. That'll bring you up to five."

"We'd be obliged. Maybe he's seen this bunch."

Jack had barely completed his sentence when the door banged open. Everyone turned to look at a tall young man carrying a short-barreled shotgun. "Marshal Ruff," the man said, "reckon you'd better come on. Looks like there's going to be trouble in the Salty Dawg. There's six rowdies at the bar creating a ruckus. I was gonna take 'em on, but I remembered what you said the last time I did, about keeping the shootin' down."

Ruff nodded at his deputy, then gave Jack a knowing glance. "It could be the men you're looking for. This here is my deputy, Gil Dixon. He's handy with a gun and don't mind using that greener he's carrying."

The town marshal turned back to Gil and introduced Jack and his deputies. Gil looked Jack over. "I've heard about you. Good work on getting those kids back."

"Thanks. Tell us about the Salty Dawg and how many men are in that bunch."

"The Salty Dawg has a front door, back door, and one side door across the saloon from the bar. Both the back door and side door have several tables between door and bar, and the saloon is full of cowhands and vaqueros tonight, plus a few citizens. The cowhands must've just been paid, 'cause there's more than usual, and the vaqueros just like to come across the river. I don't know why. Their cantinas are a lot friendlier."

Jack nodded to Gil. "Good information. Any idea where their horses are stashed?"

Gil's young face crinkled, and his lips pursed into a frown, as if thinking was a strain. "I don't know for sure, but I'd bet they're located at Rhinehart Stable. He's got the biggest sign, so most travelers pull in there, and Mr. Rhinehart does a fine job of taking care of animals."

"Good. We'll go to the stable first. I want to check their equipment. They've stolen over two hundred pounds of gold. It's got to be stashed somewhere. I wouldn't think they'd be carrying it around with them." He looked to Seth. "You ready?"

Marshal Seth Ruff stood and turned to the gunrack. He pulled the last shotgun from the rack. "I've got a couple more shotguns at my house if any of you boys would like one."

Jack shook his head. "I'm fine. Let's just get this done before they decide to move on to greener pastures."

Ruff nodded, pulled a box of shells from beneath the rack, and set it on the table. He opened it, dropped extra shells into his vest pockets, and checked the shotgun's loads. Confirming it was loaded, he snapped it shut and turned for the door.

While Ruff checked his shotgun, Jack made sure his two .44-caliber Smith and Wessons were ready. "One last word. These men killed everyone on the stage, including a woman. I'd like to bring them in and find out who tipped them about the gold and also who they're working for. However, the world won't miss these upstanding citizens. Also, if there's only six at the bar, we know there's a seventh around. Keep your eyes open. Don't let anyone suspicious get behind you." Jack shot a questioning look at Ruff. "Anything else?"

The town marshal shook his head. "Nothing except how do you want us to divvy up?"

Jack pointed at the marshal. "How about you and your deputy enter through the side door. Andy and Billy will come through the back, and I'll do the front. Hold your fire unless you see someone go for his gun. I expect if one of them tries it, and a gun is fired, they'll all join in. If that happens, you're going to have some shot-up citizens, and that's the last thing we want." Jack looked around. "Anything else?"

Four heads shook, and he headed out the door with the other lawmen following. He stepped into the street and waited until they had joined him.

Ruff stood to Jack's right with Andy to his left, followed by Billy. Gil was to Ruff's right. Several citizens saw the five men, stopped, and either slipped between the buildings, or turned and moved rapidly back up the street until jumping to the side and disappearing down an alley.

The five lawmen continued past the Salty Dawg. Seth leaned over and spoke softly to Jack. "Rhinehart Stable is the one on the left, just ahead."

Jack gave a short nod and said nothing. The five men approached the wide-open door. Stepping through, the town marshal called, "Joseph, it's Marshal Ruff."

Moments later a husky man in his mid-thirties stepped into the stable from the corral. He was wearing what, at one time, had been a white canvas apron. He lifted the end and wiped his hands, scanning the five armed men. "Goot evening, Marshal. Vat is it I can help you with?"

Jack recognized the German accent. He had learned some German from several who were in the Foreign Legion with him.

"We're looking for the horses of seven men who rode in today, probably a rough bunch."

Joseph nodded at Seth's description. "Yes. Their animals are here. They were very rude, and I was about to send them on their way when they pulled out cash to pay me up front." He shrugged. "What could I do? A man must make a living."

Jack stepped forward. "Where are their horses?"

Joseph glanced at Jack's badge. "This way, Marshal."

They followed the man to a line of stalls along the back wall of the barn. One of the stalls had a large cabinet that had a lock through the hasp.

Jack nodded toward the cabinet. "What's in that?"

"They wanted a safe place for their gear. I told them they could leave it in my office. It would be safe there, but no, they said, not safe enough, so I showed them this locker. They piled up their saddlebags inside and locked it."

Jack shoved a wide hand toward the man. "Key?"

Joseph Rhinehart shook his head. "No key. They took the only key with them. Made me swear that was the only key. I did, but it wasn't good enough for them. They searched my office before finally believing me. What do they think, their saddlebags are made of gold?"

Jack tilted his head to one side and shrugged. "Maybe."

Joseph stared at Jack like he was crazy.

Jack looked around the building. "You have a hammer?"

Joseph's eyes grew large, and the volume of his voice increased with his answer. "Yes, I do, but you can't break my lock. It is expensive. You are U.S. Marshal. I know government is slow to pay. Please don't break my lock."

Jack turned steely gray eyes on the stable owner. "I need the hammer."

The man stood his ground for a few moments longer, sighed, and marched off to another cabinet. He opened it, and Jack could see a line of tools hung neatly across the back of the locker. He spotted the hammer at the same time Joseph's thick hand wrapped around it. He lifted the heavy hammer from its hangers and gave it to Jack. He stepped to the locker and gave the lock a light tap. Nothing happened.

This time he lifted the hammer even with his shoulder and took a short swing. The lock pinged and slipped apart. He handed Joseph his hammer. The stable owner took it while staring at the destroyed lock, his lips turned down at the corners.

Ignoring the man, Jack removed the lock and yanked open

the door. Inside, seven saddlebags had been tossed on top of each other. He grabbed the top one, felt the weight of the bag, and smiled.

While he unstrapped the flap on the heavy side of the bag, Jack glanced up. "Either he's carrying enough ammunition to start a war, or there's a gold bar in this saddlebag."

He tossed the flap back, looked inside, and nodded in satisfaction. His big hand reached into the bag and extracted a bright, shiny golden bar. It glistened in the flickering light. Everyone, including Joseph Rhinehart, stared at the gleaming gold bar.

Jack hefted it. "Looks and feels like what we've been looking for, boys. Give me a hand checking these others." He handed the bags toward the watching men and grabbed another one. Within minutes they were opened, and the gold was accounted for.

Jack turned to the stable owner. "Mr. Rhinehart, we need two things. First, we need a place to stash this gold. Then you need to leave. I feel sure we'll catch all of the bandits, but if one happens to get away and comes back here, you don't want to be here."

"Yeah, Mr. Marshal. I understand. There is a safe in my office. You can put it there, but if you would take it out as soon as possible, I would be most happy. That's too much money. People kill for that kind of money."

Jack nodded to Rhinehart. "They have. At the latest, we'll have it out of here in a couple of hours. By the way, how much was that lock I broke?"

Rhinehart shook his head. "It was three dollars, but there's no need for you to make a report. I will never see the money."

Jack dug in his vest pocket. Finding what he was looking for, he pulled out a quarter eagle and dropped it into the man's outstretched hand. "I'm with you, Joseph. I don't think much of the government when it comes to paying its bills. This'll take care of your loss." He turned to the deputies. "Let's move the gold to Mr. Rhinehart's safe. Then we'll stack these saddlebags back in the locker. We'll put what's left of the lock on it." The men made short work of the bags and the gold. When they were finished, Jack and the others waited for Rhinehart to lock up and head for home. Once he was gone, they headed for the saloon. Nothing had changed. The piano was banging away, a dancehall girl was singing, and the sound of revelry filled the streets.

Reaching the Salty Dawg, the four men split off, two heading for the side door and two to the back. Jack walked to the saloon front and halted at the batwing doors. Silently, he examined the interior and patrons.

The saloon looked like so many other western saloons. A bar ran along the right side, this one looked to be about thirty feet long, tables were to the left, and gaming tables in the back. Raucous laughter echoed through the smoke-filled watering hole. Occasionally a shout or curse would rise from someone at the gaming tables, reflecting a win or loss.

Jack directed his gaze toward the bar. To his surprise, he recognized one of the outlaws. The blond-headed man was drinking a beer and laughing around it at what one of his companions had said. It was Blondie from the hanging. His unkempt long blond hair hung to his shoulders, and Jack remembered him enjoying the hanging almost as much as Vern had.

Jack, unconsciously, lifted one hand to his neck while the other brushed the butt of his six-gun. The fingers at his neck ran lightly over the still puffy scars circling his throat. *You've got a surprise coming to you, Blondie,* Jack thought. *So it is the Rush gang doing these robberies. Rush uses his cattle ranch as a smoke screen. The distance and the rugged terrain surrounding his ranch are perfect cover, convincing the locals he couldn't be guilty. But how do they get rid of the gold? They've got to have an outlet either here or across the border. There's no way they could have managed to get the first load back to their ranch. A wagon could never make that trip, and a string of pack mules would have been spotted.*

Jack pushed the doors wide and stepped through. He moved to his right, to get the wall behind him. Not that the thin wall would provide any protection, but it did give him concealment from anyone who might be in the street. Once his back was covered, he stopped, standing silent, watching and waiting. All of the gang were along the bar, drinking and laughing.

The side door opened. Marshal Ruff and Deputy Gil stepped into the saloon, both carrying shotguns, and began easing toward the bar. With each table they passed, they motioned toward the door. Patrons jumped to their feet and made a quick but quiet exit from the saloon.

At the same time, the back door eased open. Andy and Billy walked through and leveled their six-guns at the men along the bar. All four lawmen light-footed it toward the bar until they were less than twenty feet from the killers. Patrons were slipping, as quietly as possible, through the front, side, and back doors. Gradually the din of the saloon decreased until the only sound was the piano and the laughter of the six men at the bar.

They must really be drunk, Jack thought. Finally, Blondie swung unsteadily around. As he turned, he hooked his boot heel over the foot brace running along the length of the bar, and started to lean back, elbows against the top surface.

At the sight of Jack, he froze, elbows in midair. His body, already in motion, thudded against the bar. With eyelids spread wide and eyes bugging out, he gaped at Jack. Seeing the man he had hanged was almost more than he could take, but next, his eyes caught sight of the four men, two with shotguns. His mouth worked several times before any words made it out. Blondie's tongue darted to lick his suddenly dry lips, his head swiveling to stare at Jack and the other four lawmen. He couldn't keep those shiny blue eyes off the big man who was supposed to be dead. Now that same dead man stood silently at the end of the bar, like an apparition. Blondie at last broke the trance he was in and slammed his elbow into the man next to him.

18

Grunting with shock from the jab of the sharp elbow, the gunman turned to curse Blondie. Something must have tipped him off, maybe the empty saloon, or the shotguns pointing at his belly, or the five men, guns drawn, all aimed at him. He spun further around, going into a crouch, but he was so drunk he lost his balance. Staggering for a second, he appeared as if he couldn't make up his mind whether to grab for his gun or break his fall. Finally, completely losing his balance, breaking his fall jumped to the front of his list. On his way down, he caught the edge of a chair with his gun hand. Unfortunately for him, he was so out of kilter the chair went with him and clattered to the floor along with his drunken body.

The remaining four men, still unaware of what or who they were up against, broke into laughter and turned to watch their pardner's drunken struggles, only to find multiple gun barrels trained on them. When they had all turned, Jack was shocked to see the Rush kid he had killed in the courtroom so many days ago. But it wasn't the one he had killed, it was Vern, the twin brother. The one who had been at the other end of the rope as Jack hung choking to death. The boy's face turned ashen when his eyes fell on the man he thought was dead. The man he had hanged.

Jack waved a six-gun toward the fella on the floor. "One of you help him up."

No one moved. Jack pointed his .44 at a tall lanky outlaw in the middle of the gang. "You. Pick him up."

The man, singled out, moved quickly to help the drunk to his feet, and leaned him against the bar.

Jack, staying clear of the muzzles of his companions, moved sideways among the tables to slip in front of the six men, giving him a better angle should he have to shoot. "I want all of you to slowly, using your off hand, unfasten the buckle of your gun belt and let it fall to the floor."

Only one man moved. It was Blondie. His left hand did exactly as he was told. He unfastened the gun belt and let it drop. "I dropped my gun, Marshal. You can see that." He thrust both hands as high as he could reach above his head. "You can see. I ain't trying to draw a gun against you."

Vern, a sneer lifting one corner of his thin lips, said, "You ain't nothin' but a yellow-belly coward, Milt. You're fired."

Milt returned the sneer. "I may be a yellow-belly coward, Vern, but I'm gonna be a live coward, while you'll just be dead on the floor."

Jack's hard voice boomed through the now silent saloon. "Listen to him, boys. He knows what he's talking about. Don't even think about opening this ball. You've got two shotguns pointed at you, and three more six-guns. Either drop those guns or get ready to meet the devil. Now!"

The remainder of the gun belts hit the floor except for the drunk and Vern.

Vern's color had yet to recover. In fact, his face was so pale, he looked as if there weren't a drop of blood remaining in it. He continued to stare at Jack with fear-filled blue eyes. "If'n I drop my gun, Sage, you're gonna kill me. I know it."

The drunk, leaning against the bar and weaving from side to side, yelled, causing everyone to jump. "Kill him, Vern. Gutshoot him. If you don't, he'll shoot you fer sure."

Jack was tempted to shoot the drunk, but kept his eyes on Vern. "Listen to me, Vern, I won't kill you. You'll get a fair trial just like everyone else, but if you draw, I will kill you, and I'll enjoy doing it. I'm telling you for the last time. Drop your gun."

Vern's right hand hovered over his gun for a moment longer, at last the hand slowly relaxed, and his left moved to the buckle of his gun belt. He unbuckled and eased his six-gun down. The weapon softly touched the floor, and Vern released the belt, allowing it to drop into the sawdust.

Jack stepped forward just as the drunk went for his gun. It was a sad showing. The drunken man's hand fumbled his initial draw, found the butt of his gun, and closed around it. His self-satisfied grin disappeared from his face when Jack's big fist collided with his jaw. The drunk stiffened, and his eyes rolled back. His body stretched to his full height, pivoted slowly to his left, and fell to his right, crashing to the floor. Andy stepped forward and stripped the gun belt from the unconscious man's body, tossing it on a nearby table. Ruff and his deputy, Gil, moved closer.

Jack asked, "Which one of you men is Ted?" All were silent.

Andy spoke up. "Jack, he's not here. I know all these men, and he's not one of them. If you remember, Lester Nelson, the sheriff in Mesilla, said Ted was jawing about a girl named Rosita. Maybe he's visiting her."

"Probably right." Jack turned to Ruff. "Do you know a saloon girl named Rosita?"

Ruff shook his head. "I know several, but she may not be any of them. Look where you are. Rosita's a popular name around here. It's no tellin' where she might be. Gil, you have any ideas?"

The deputy nodded. "Marshal, there's a Rosita who works right here, but she wasn't working when I looked in before I came after you, and she wasn't in the bunch of girls who got out of here. I'll tell you, though, this Rosita is about the best-looking woman this side of the border. She might not have anything to do with the Ted Rush feller, but if he picks lookers, she's the one."

"Alright," Jack said. "Andy, you know this guy, and Gil, you know Rosita, why don't you two come with me, and we'll go look for her." He turned to Ruff. "Marshal, do you mind taking this bunch, with Billy, to your jail and locking them up? It'll be a while. I'll have to get a message to Judge Coleman to see where he wants them sent." He nodded at Blondie, who had surrendered so easily. "If you've got the space, you'd best put Blondie in a cell by himself. He doesn't look to be too popular."

Several of the killers were glaring at the blond man.

"Sure." The marshal waved his shotgun toward the drunk. His low voice was threatening. "Pick up your friend."

Three men stepped forward and picked the unconscious man up, one at each shirt cuff and one at his feet.

Jack glanced at Gil. "You know where she lives?"

"Nope, I sure don't, but I'll guarantee you Blakeslee, the bartender, does. He runs this place and knows where everyone who works here lives."

Jack waved the bartender over. "Where can I find Rosita?"

Blakeslee didn't hesitate. He gave Jack detailed instructions on how and where to find the girl.

Jack watched the killers being marched from the saloon. Ted Rush was on his mind. He wanted the ringleader of this bunch in his hands before any more time passed. *He's the reason the lady was assaulted and killed,* Jack thought. *Rush could have stopped those men and only taken the gold, but he didn't. It's time for him to pay.*

Gil led them near the river where there were several small adobe homes under tall cottonwood trees. A soft breeze brought the cry of crickets chirping in the grass and children playing in the light cast from candles and lanterns. Voices carried from both sides of the river, laughter from the children, and conversations of men and women. A guitar strummed, and a lullaby of a mother to her baby floated on the night air.

"Here," Gil said softly. He stopped in front of one of the small adobe homes. No lights showed from inside the house. An occasional cluck from the north side of the building indicated the location of Rosita's chicken coop. A dog barked in the distance.

Jack grasped Gil's shoulder. "Cover the back." To Andy, he motioned to follow. After waiting long enough to allow Gil to slip around the chicken coop, Jack drove his foot against the front door.

It might as well not have been latched, for the door slammed open, and Jack crashed inside. He stepped into the room, his eyes searching for bodies and movement. Spotting the occupied bed and the man raised up in it, he reached out, grabbed him around the throat, and dragged him across the screaming woman. Squeezing tighter, he yanked Rush erect in front of him.

Jack caught the flash of the knife in time to block the swing. His big hand closed around the wrist. Rush was not a small man, but against Jack he stood no chance. Jack squeezed and twisted the wrist, bones cracked audibly, and Rush screamed. The knife fell harmlessly to the floor.

But Rush wasn't a quitter. Curses spewed from his mouth, and he managed to land a blow on Jack's forehead. The big lawman, still gripping the outlaw's throat, turned and threw Rush through the front door, past Andy, into the yard. There was a small mesquite-limb fence around the yard. Rush crashed into it. His body tore through the limbs of the fence while sharp, dried mesquite thorns drove into his hips and legs. At the same time, his feet tangled in the limbs, causing him to sprawl across the fence.

Neighbors, carrying lanterns, rushed out of their houses to check on the commotion. The light illuminated Rush's right hand and wrist, now uselessly limp, the fingers twitching. Jack strode into the yard. Rush cursed him and kicked at him when he was close, but his bare foot did no damage, glancing harmlessly off the lawman's shin.

Jack bent and grabbed the killer as he was trying to get to his feet. In the east corner of the yard, a large oak tree stood silently observing. Jack threw Rush against the rough bark of the oak's thick trunk. The whoosh of his breath shooting from his lungs could be heard by all. Rush lay gasping for air. Seeing Jack approach, he staggered to his feet and tried a left, but Jack flicked it away with his right forearm and slapped the outlaw with the open palm of his left hand. The crack sounded like a six-gun firing, and Rush's head snapped to his left.

He jumped for Jack and sank his teeth into the lawman's right bicep. Jack grabbed the man's hair, yanked his head back, tearing him loose, and smashed a right to Rush's face. The killer's nose flattened, and blood spurted in all directions.

Rosita, her robe pulled tight around her, dashed from the house, but Gil grabbed her by the arm and held her at the doorway.

Rush was bucking, trying to get out of Jack's grip, and cursing him through bloody lips. Jack, his fist still gripping Rush's hair, held him at arm's length. His voice was low, gravelly, and threatening. "You killed all those people and that woman for money. You're worse than the lowest scum on this earth."

By the lantern light, Jack could see the hate-filled eyes glaring at him. "I'll kill you for this. You can't treat a Rush this way and live."

"We'll just have to see about that," Jack said, and released a driving right fist into the man's face. He felt Rush go limp, and released his grip on Rush's hair, allowing the killer to collapse into the Texas dirt.

Blood covered his hands, and his bicep was bleeding from where Rush had sunk his teeth. He bent to the ground and scooped a handful of dirt, rubbing it over his hands to clean them, then turned to Gil and Andy. "Let's get this scum to the jail."

Gil nodded. "You probably need to get the doc to look at that bite."

Andy grinned. "Yeah, I've heard the bite from a human is worse than a mad dog. Especially from that mouth, after what I heard coming out of it."

Gil looked at the horrified woman beside him. "Go inside, and stay away from his kind."

She stared across the yard at Jack. "He will kill you, him or his family. You have done worse to him than if you had shot him. Word will go around quickly."

Jack touched his hand to his Stetson. "Ma'am." He turned to Andy. "Grab a foot." He bent and picked up one foot, Andy the other.

Gil stood next to Andy. "You gonna drag him all the way to jail? It gets pretty rocky betwixt here and there."

Jack, Rush's foot in his hand, started forward. "He's welcome to walk any time he wants."

Andy grabbed the other foot and glanced at Jack. "What's the plan now?"

"To get a good night's rest. The animals need it as much as we do."

Halfway back to the jail, Rush awoke. His initial moans quickly turned to yells.

"You're killin' me. Let me up."

Jack threw the foot to the ground, followed by Andy. "Get up."

Rush moaned again. "I think you broke my ribs when you threw me against that blamed tree. I don't think I can walk."

Jack said nothing. He bent over, grabbed a foot, and started off.

"Wait, wait. You'll kill me draggin' my head across these rocks."

Jack stopped, still holding the man's foot. "You either walk, or we drag you, your choice."

Rush moaned again. "But my boots are back at Rosita's place. I can't walk without them."

"Walk or be dragged. Make up your mind." Jack waited another second and took a step forward. Rush's back scraped across the rocky and thorny ground.

"Alright, alright. I'll walk, just let me up."

Jack threw the man's foot down for the second time, stepped back, and waited. He watched as the bleeding outlaw struggled to his feet. Once erect, Rush momentarily staggered, trying to maintain his balance.

He glared at Jack. "You're gonna pay for this."

Jack shoved the man forward. "Get moving."

Gil glanced down at the man's bare feet. "You want me to go back and get his boots?"

Jack said nothing.

"Jack?"

"It makes no difference to me. If you want to, go ahead. We can find our own way to the jail."

Undecided, Gil shifted from one foot to the other, then turned toward Rosita's place. "I'll get his boots."

In response, Jack gave Rush another shove.

"Easy," Rush snapped. "I told you my ribs are broken. Ouch!" He stopped to pull a goathead sticker from his foot, and Jack gave him a harder shove. This time, he almost fell, but managed to get his foot to the ground in time to keep from slamming onto the rocks. "You're a mighty impatient man."

Jack said nothing. He was having dark thoughts about the woman Rush had killed. *You abused and killed that woman and those other folks on the stage. You don't deserve to live. I should shoot you where you stand, and probably every one of your gang.* His hand caressed the butt of his Smith and Wesson. *Killing this snake would be no loss to the world,* he thought. *He contributes nothing. Unlike wolves and bears, they kill only when they need to eat, feed their young, or protect themselves. Rush kills for pleasure. His kind is not needed on this earth.* He paused, gray eyes locked on Rush. His hand dropped away from his revolver. *But the law is. The sooner law comes to this land, the better.*

He heard running feet and looked back. It was Gil with the outlaw's boots.

"You want to stop and let him put his boots on?"

Rush stopped, and Jack gave him another hard shove. "Keep moving. No one said you could stop."

"But he's got my boots."

"Yep, and you'll get them when we get to the office, not before."

Rush staggered forward. "But my feet . . ."

"Your feet will wait."

Rush picked up a grass burr in his left foot and tried to pause to get it out, but Jack shoved him forward. "Stop one more time, and I'll drag you the rest of the way."

Gil stared at Jack while Rush cursed softly under his breath. Then the outlaw said, "My time will come, Sage, and you'll regret this."

"Your time has already come and gone, and I already regret it. I should have shot you when you pulled that knife on me. Now shut up. I'm tired of listening to your bellyaching."

They came to the marshal's office, and Gil opened the door. Rush walked in, leaving bloody footprints across the floor.

Ruff, sitting behind his desk, watched the bloodied and bruised outlaw.

Billy sat in a chair against the wall, drinking a cup of coffee. He looked Rush over and switched to Jack. "Looks like you're bleeding from your arm there, Jack. Want me to get the doctor for you?"

Rush, whose nose was flattened against his right cheek with

blood all over his face, chest, and feet, glanced at Jack. "What about me? I'm in a lot worse shape than he is."

Andy spoke up. "You shouldn't have attacked him with your knife. He don't like knives."

Jack looked at the gunsmith turned deputy. The man grinned back at him. "Well, do you?"

Jack shook his head and turned to the marshal. "You have a cell for this one? This is Ted Rush, the leader of this bunch."

Marshal Ruff glanced at Gil. "Go get the doc. Looks like he's gonna be needed."

Gil frowned. "He ain't gonna be happy about being woke up this time of night."

The marshal held Gil's gaze.

His eyebrows rose. "Guess that's why I'm the deputy." He turned and headed out the open door, pulling it closed behind him.

The marshal turned back to Jack. "He put up a little tussle?"

"Not much, I just don't care for his kind."

Ruff stood, grabbed his keys, and motioned for Rush to follow him.

Rush whined at the marshal. "What about the doctor? I need help."

Marshal Ruff grabbed Rush's arm. "He can see you in a cell as easily as he can see you out here. Now get in there."

Jack watched as the marshal shoved Rush through the main door into the cell block. Keys turned in cell door locks. Moments later he was back. Jack nodded toward the cells. "You mind keeping those fellas until the judge decides where he'll have the trials? I'm sure it'll be in either Silver City or Socorro. The prison wagon will pick them up."

"Not at all. Of course, New Mexico Territory will have to reimburse us for the expense of guarding and feeding these fine gentlemen."

Jack shook his head. "Won't be a problem. You shouldn't have them very long. Judge Coleman will want to make an example of this bunch as soon as possible. That'll include old man Rush and the men at the ranch. You don't get too popular when you rob gold-carrying stages and kill passengers."

Jack looked toward the cells. "Speaking of that, we need a witness to clinch this. How about if I take one of those fine fellas outside for a bit, and we can have a talk. How's that sound to you?"

The marshal nodded. "I saw your work when you were chasing the kidnappers of those girls. You can be mighty persuasive, but you'll need a quiet place to work, and I've got just the place. The attorney's office next door. I keep an eye on it for him when he's out of town, and it just so happens he's away for a few days." Ruff frowned at Jack. "Try not to get it bloody. I don't want to have to clean it up."

19

Jack opened the lawyer's office door and shoved Blondie in. "Pull those shades," he said to Andy and Billy. The two men lowered the shades over the front window and the small etched glass window of the door. Once they were down, Jack lit the lamp and turned to Blondie, who was standing in front of the lawyer's desk, his wide eyes locked on Jack.

Jack indicated a straight-backed wooden chair adjacent to a file cabinet. "Grab that chair. Move it in front of the desk and sit."

The outlaw's hand was shaking when he extended it to grasp the back of the chair. He pulled it to where Jack indicated, sat, and stared up at the giant lawman, his eyes wide, like a dog that knew he was in trouble.

Jack slowly pulled his Bowie knife from its belt scabbard and shaved a few hairs from the back of his hand. When he was finished, he laid the knife on the desk, in reach of both him and the outlaw. He locked the frightened man in a cold stare. "What's your name?"

"It's Milt, Marshal, Milt Haggard."

"Milt," Jack said, staring at a fly on the lampshade. "Milt

Haggard." He turned to his two deputies. "You boys heard of that name?"

Andy shook his head. "Nope, it ain't familiar to me."

Billy nodded. "I have. Seen it on a circular when I was deputy for the sheriff in Silver City. Yes, sir. There's a fifty-dollar reward for him. Don't remember what he did. Can't be too much for only fifty bucks."

Jack looked back at Milt. "Sounds like you're a wanted man, Milt. How'd that happen?" Jack's goal was to get the man talking about anything. Once he was answering questions, it would make it easier for him to answer the more important ones.

"It weren't nothin' much, Marshal, sir."

Jack nodded. "Tell me about it, Milt."

The blond outlaw shook his head. "Happened quite a while ago. Back around the St. Louis area. A swindling gambler tried to cheat me out of a hand of poker, and I just rightly stuck him with my Arkansas toothpick. It was a righteous act. He was a thief."

"If he was the thief, how is it you've got a reward out on your head?"

"Well, sir, he was also the mayor's brother-in-law. I got my money and hightailed it out of town, caught up with a wagon train headed for Santa Fe, and here I am."

Jack had pulled the chair's twin in front of Milt. He had the back turned toward the man and sat facing the outlaw, his arms crossed over the top of the wooden back. "Now here you are. I think you'll agree this isn't stabbing a cheating gambler, is it?"

His face solemn, the man shook his head. "No, sir, it sure isn't. I don't know how I managed to get myself into such a spot as this. I just joined up with the wrong folks."

Milt flinched away from Jack when he jerked his left hand to his bandanna. He waited while the outlaw slowly straightened, and yanked the bandanna from around his neck, exposing the still red and swollen rope scar in his flesh. His voice rose. "Did those 'wrong folks' make you do this? Did those 'wrong folks' make you kill those people on the stage? Tell me, Milt, did those 'wrong folks' make you rape and beat Silver City's schoolmarm, old Mrs. Graves?"

While talking with Jack, Milt Haggard had slowly relaxed. The tremors had left his hands while he had spoken about St. Louis, but now sweat popped out on his forehead, and his head rotated back and forth, looking at each of the lawmen. His tongue flicked out, licking his lips, while his entire body began to shake. "I swear, Marshal Sage, I didn't want to throw that rope, and I sure didn't want to see you hang, but if'n I hadn't, they would have surely hanged me right then and there."

Jack leaned forward against the back of the chair, bringing the front legs off the floor and putting his face within inches of Haggard. "Did they make you kill those people on the stage and do what you did to Mrs. Graves? Did they, Milt?"

Tears edged at the corners of the man's eyes. He was shaking so badly he bounced in the chair. "I swear I didn't want to. Ted and Vern made me do it. I swear they did. I liked Mrs. Graves. She was always nice to me in Silver City."

Jack leaned back, easing the front legs of his chair to the floor, and waited while Milt Haggard calmed down. After several minutes he asked, "How many people are at the ranch?"

"Eight, Marshal, there's eight counting Elijah."

Jack could see the man was relieved to be talking about anything except his part in the hanging and the stage robbery. "Do they stay around the ranch house or work the cattle?"

"Nobody's working cattle. They're all at the ranch. Elijah, his boys, and Durant sleep in the main house. The rest of us are in the bunkhouse."

"When are they expecting you back from this holdup?"

Milt was calming down again. "When they see us. The old man knows his boys need to blow off steam, and he lets 'em do it. He usually gives us a few days out. We were going to be heading back tomorrow after we cashed in the gold."

"Is that what you did with the other gold?"

Haggard hesitated and looked at the floor.

"Don't lie to me, Milt. I've been doing this a long time. I'll know if you're lying, and it won't go well for you."

The outlaw nodded. "Yes, sir, Mr. Marshal. That's what we did. It's a lot easier to carry paper money than it is to haul around gold."

"So all that money is at the ranch house?"

"Yes, sir. Don't know where, except Elijah keeps it somewhere in the house. He don't trust many people."

Jack stood and stretched his back. "Who was leading the other holdup?"

Relaxed and trying to ingratiate himself, Milt continued to spill the beans. "Why, the same crew, with Ted and Vern leading. Ted's really the boss man, but Vern's mighty touchy. You got to be careful with him. He's got a hair trigger, so Ted, most of the time, lets him think he's leading, too."

Jack looked first at Andy, who was standing by the door, and Billy, who had been sitting at the attorney's desk behind Milt, writing everything the outlaw said. "You boys have anything to ask Milt?"

Andy spoke up. "Who planned the robberies?"

Milt answered looking directly at Jack. "It was Elijah Rush and Micah Durant. They've been together a long time. The old man would ask Ted's opinion occasionally, but never Vern's."

"Milt," Jack said, "did Ted or Vern order the killing of all those people in both robberies?"

Milt shook his head but said, "Yes and no. Ted ordered it, but Elijah told him to. We all heard him before we left. He said to make sure no one survived so there'd be no witnesses."

"Alright. Now all we need is for you to sign your statement, and we'll witness it."

Milt Haggard stood and walked around the desk, passing the Bowie knife. Jack watched the man eye the knife. Haggard shot

Jack a furtive glance, saw him watching, jerked his eyes away, and stepped up to Billy.

"Where do I sign?"

Billy showed him, and the man bent over the paper, gripping the pen so hard his nails turned white. His tongue edged to the corner of his mouth, and he laid his arm around the top of the paper to block the sight of anyone who might be watching. After a long minute he rose. "Will that do?"

Jack looked at the man's signature, a jagged X. "That'll do just fine. You've done good, Milt." He leaned over, took the pen, dipped it, and signed his name beneath Milt's X, then returned it to Billy, who signed beneath him. Andy added the last signature to the confession, and Billy blew softly on the paper, drying the ink.

Jack watched hope fill the eyes of the bloodthirsty killer.

"Does this mean I won't hang?"

Jack stooped so he could look straight into the man's eyes and let the disgust he felt for this man flood his voice. "No, it doesn't mean you won't hang, you lowlife. You killed innocent people and beat an old woman to death." Jack pointed to the scar on his neck. "Get a good look at this. Your neck is going to look exactly like mine, except you won't be able to see it. You'll be dead."

Shock raced across Haggard's face. His complexion turned gray, and he started to throw up on the attorney's floor. Jack grabbed him by the collar. In two long strides he had him through the door and threw him into the street, where the killer landed on his hands and knees. His body shook as he vomited the liquor and whatever food remained into the dirt street. He retched again and again. Jack watched for only a moment.

The satisfaction he had felt telling the man he was going to hang was gone. Watching him on his hands and knees in the manure-filled dirt of the El Paso street brought only gloom. *I should hate you, Blondie,* he thought, *but I can't help but feel a touch of pity for anyone who's so eaten up with fear. How'd you end up here?*

Did you have a harder life than others who became good citizens? Were you just a spoiled kid who got his way with everything? You're big enough, maybe you were a bully, but if you were, your bullying days are over. These next months won't repay Mrs. Graves and the other people who were murdered, but they'll surely be miserable for you.

He shook his head and turned to Billy, who was stepping out of the attorney's office with Milt's signed confession. Both Andy and Billy were somber watching the outlaw.

"Jack," Billy said, "reckon I ain't ever seen anyone give away information like Milt did. I'm guessin' you've done this before."

"Time or two," Jack said and nodded toward Haggard. "I'll be with Marshal Ruff when he's finished. Get him some water or something to settle his stomach, then bring him in. Once he's locked up, we'll get some sleep."

Billy nodded. "I can use it."

Ruff looked up from his desk as Jack entered the office. "You get anything?"

Jack motioned with his head, and Ruff rose. The two men stepped outside and closed the office door. Jack held out the confession. In the light spilling from his window, Ruff read Billy's transcription of Haggard's words. When he was done, he let out a low whistle and handed the papers back to Jack.

"Looks like Milt put a noose around every man's neck involved. If you catch 'em all, this'll be the most men ever hanged at one time in the territory. Though they deserve it, I'm glad I don't have to be there to watch." As he spoke, he saw the scar around Jack's neck. "That's new."

"Yep, compliments of Elijah Rush and a few of those folks in your jail."

"And you're here, upright and breathing. I'm bettin' that's quite a story."

Haggard was staggering to his knees, still weak from the shock and vomiting. A horse trough was in front of the marshal's office, along with a bucket. Billy dipped the bucket into the trough and sloshed Milt with a bucketful of water, getting most of the residue off the man. He handed the outlaw the bucket and allowed him to drink. Milt held it to his mouth, water running around the corners. Finished, he gave it to Billy, who motioned him toward the jail.

Marshal Ruff stepped back to let them pass. "Whew, he does stink. There'll be some almighty complaining coming from my residents in just a second." He followed, unlocking and shoving Milt through the cell block door and down to the empty cell.

Vern called, "Marshal, don't put that puke-covered coward in here. We cain't stand the stink."

The other men chimed in, but Ruff ignored them, locking Milt Haggard in the one cell that remained empty. The marshal stepped through the cellblock door, locked it, and turned to Jack. "What's your plans now?"

"A night's rest, then we hit the trail. Haggard gave us enough information to put an end to Elijah Rush's reign. I aim to see him stand before Judge Coleman. It's time justice came to roost on that man's shoulders."

Ruff extended his hand. "We'll take care of your prisoners until the wagon shows up. Don't you worry about them. Good luck to you."

Jack took the offered hand. "I'm obliged. This is twice you've helped me. You ever need anything from me, anything, let me know. I'll come running."

Ruff nodded. "Just doin' my job."

Jack motioned toward the door. Billy and Andy followed. Across the street was the Traveler's Rest hotel. Jack pulled his watch from his vest pocket, his thumb running over the emerald set in the cover. He flipped it up and checked the time in the light from the marshal's window. "Boys, it's close to eleven. If you want to grab a bite, go ahead, but I'm putting this old bag of bones in a bed right now. We'll need to pick up supplies and ammunition in the morning. I'll be putting on the feedbag about six. If you're interested, meet me then."

Jack nodded, tapped the brim of his hat to his two men, and headed for the hotel. He was tired. It was a good and bad tired. They had successfully taken down half of Elijah Rush's bunch and reclaimed the gold. Unfortunately there was no way to bring Mrs. Graves or the other stage passengers back to life, but at least their murderers would meet justice.

He crossed the wide, dusty street in and out of shafts of light slanting from the few lit windows. Reaching the hotel steps, he paused, glancing at the nearby saloon. *I could eat something,* he thought, but shook his head, climbed the steps, and pushed open the door of the Traveler's Rest. *This is what I need more than food.*

The clerk looked up from his ledger. "Can I help you, sir?"

"You sure can, mister," and Jack reached for the ledger.

JACK COULD FEEL the tiredness in Smokey and Stonewall. He'd leave them both at Tiny's livery when they got back to Silver City. It would be either Pepper's or Thunder's turn for the final ride out to the Triple Six Ranch. If Marshal Hardwick wanted to put together a posse, it was fine with him. This was one of those times that it might actually come in handy to have a large number of men, as long as they didn't get trigger-happy.

Billy and Andy had been quiet for the last couple of hours. They were nearing Silver City. The mules and horses weren't the only ones tired. An additional two mules had been rented to carry the gold.

The three men dropped off the rolling plains of the Chihuahuan desert, descending along a slope toward the Mimbres River.

Billy straightened as they neared the river. "That water'll taste mighty good."

Jack said nothing, and Andy responded, "I just want to get off this horse and out of this saddle."

Nearing the outer edge of the tall cottonwoods, the land leveled. The cottonwood trees, willows, and salt cedars extended at least fifty yards on both sides of the river.

Jack couldn't stand the salt cedar. It made him sneeze, but it would be nice to taste some fresh water and stretch his legs, especially the right one. That bullet in his thigh from so long ago still bothered him. It hadn't broken any bones, but he figured it must have done quite a bit of damage to the muscle, since it caused the leg to cramp and stiffen when he rode for long periods of time.

The trees were thick along this part of the river. With the angle of the sun, it was hard to see under the canopy. They had been cautious, watching for Apache, hoping if there were any, they'd see them before the Indians spotted them.

Jack was beginning to relax when he saw movement under the trees. Moments later fifty or so Apaches on horseback charged out from the shadows, surrounding them, rifles and bows trained on the three lawmen.

"Easy," Jack said to the two deputies, "maybe they're not feeling too bloody today. Don't give them a reason to change their mind."

Andy grunted as the Indians neared. "Never seen 'em when they weren't feelin' bloody."

Jack nodded to his captors. "Howdy. What can I do for you?"

From the shadow of a near cottonwood, Victorio rode out. "Jack Sage. You are looking much better than you were when last we met. How is your neck?"

Jack took a deep breath. "Still holding my head up, Chief." He slowly reached for the bandanna, watching the muzzles and arrows track his movement, and yanked it off, exposing the almost healed scar.

Victorio pushed his horse through the riders and sidled up to Jack. He reached his hand out and felt the puffy flesh of Jack's neck. "You have permanently been marked by the Rush men. Will you do something about that?"

Jack nodded. "Oh yeah. I've already caught a bunch of them. They robbed the stage and killed the passengers."

"Yes," Victorio said, "we saw the tracks of them and you. They tried to make it look like it was my people who made the attack, but you figured it out."

"I did with the help of these two, my friends, and also with their help, we caught them in El Paso. They will go to one of our trials, and they will hang for what they did."

Victorio nodded. "Good. What about the others? What will you do with them?"

Jack thought, *I might as well tell him, maybe he knows something and can help us, or maybe he'll let us pass. If he doesn't, we're all dead, so it makes no difference.*

"That is where we're headed right now. First to Silver City and then to Rush's ranch. We will take him and his henchmen, and they will be tried and hanged with their friends."

Victorio gave a firm nod. "That is good. They are bad men and should die." The chief gave Jack a long look. "I think I should let my men kill you, Jack Sage. I would not want you for an enemy."

Jack grinned at the chief. "I sure prefer you didn't, Victorio. I've got plans and people who need to be brought to justice. But let me assure you, I am not your enemy. You saved my life, and I owe you. I pay my debts. Anytime you need my help, you let me know. But I must say the truth to you. If you harm my people's families unjustly, I might be forced to come after you. I do not say this with any anger or pride, only with truth."

The chief, erect and solemn, stared at Jack. "I see your truth. You are strong. Like me, you do not fear death. I would be honored to fight alongside you or against you, but today, we have peace, and I will tell you one thing about Elijah Rush's ranch house.

"It is built close to the north canyon wall. It cannot be attacked except from the south, but a man with courage can use a rope to get down the side of the canyon to the house. On that side, there is a window. It is possible a man might slip through the window. It is also possible the man might be killed slipping through the window. Like I said, it would take a man of courage. Good fortune with your justice, Jack Sage."

"Thanks, and to you, Chief Victorio."

Victorio said something in Apache to his braves. The horsemen separated, making a hole for Jack and his men to ride through. Jack gave a nod to Victorio and clucked to Smokey. The grulla started forward with Stonewall crowding close. Billy and Andy were also close behind.

Jack felt the crawlies between his shoulders, but held Smokey to a slow walk as they proceeded to the graveled edge of the fast-running river.

Suddenly, Victorio wheeled his horse, let out a whoop, and dashed past them, followed by his shrieking band. The Apaches splashed across the Mimbres, up the opposite slope, and disappeared over the ridgeline.

Andy was the first to speak. He let out a long breath. "At first, when they came out of the trees, I thought we were dead. Then when they charged us, I knew we were dead. That's about the closest I've ever been to meeting my maker. We wouldn't have had a snowball's chance." He turned and gazed at Jack. "You looked as cool as a mountain stream. How'd you do that?"

Jack gave a short laugh. "My stomach was churning, but you can't show fear. Do that, and you're dead. I learned that little secret a long time ago and a long way from here. Why don't we give these fine animals a drink, and maybe us too."

20

F etter rushed from his office, the first to greet the three riders. "Did you get the gold?"

I'm developing a real dislike for this fella, Jack thought. He swung down from Smokey, flipped the reins around the hitching rail, and pushed his hat back. Staring down at Fetter, he could barely see the man's eyes for the green visor the Wells Fargo agent was wearing. "Yeah, Fetter, we got your gold." He motioned to Billy and Andy. They tossed him the reins of the two mules and dismounted. In turn he tossed the reins to Fetter. "I want a signed receipt for the gold and the mules. They belong to the Butterfield Stage Company and are to be returned to them. If not, Wells Fargo will be getting a substantial bill."

Fetter caught the reins, turned, and yelled into his office, "Davis, get out here." A young man of no more than seventeen, a larger copy of Fetter, green visor included, dashed out the office door.

"Yes, sir?"

Fetter pointed to the packs. "Get those into the office, and make it quick." He leaned close to the young man and said in a whisper, "There's gold in those packs. Don't be obvious." He shot a suspicious glance at two young women passing the office.

"Yes, sir," Davis replied, taking the reins and tying the mules to an adjacent hitching rail. He began untying the packs.

Fetter turned back to Jack. "Is it all there?"

Jack handed Fetter a statement signed by the Wells Fargo office in El Paso, warranting the amount of gold Jack had captured.

Fetter read it carefully and allowed a smile to drift across his face. "At least we've gotten this back in its entirety." His head jerked up to stare at Jack. "Do you know anything about the previous stolen shipment?"

"Do you know if Marshal Hardwick is in town?"

"Why, yes. I do believe he is, and about the first shipment?"

"I'll be reporting to the marshal. You can check with him." He turned to Billy and Andy. "Mount up, boys. Take your horses to Tiny's." He rubbed Smokey between the ears. "I'm betting they're mighty tired and hungry. How about taking Smokey and Stonewall? I'm heading for the marshal's office." He tossed their reins to Andy.

Andy caught them as he and Billy stepped back into their saddles. Billy let out a long yawn. "They ain't the onliest ones. I feel like I could sleep for a week."

Jack shook his head. "Grab something to eat. We're going to be pulling out as soon as I meet with the marshal. I'll meet you at the Gold Strike Hotel. Eat there, and I'll put it on my tab. I've got to change clothes and pick up some clean ones to take with me. You're welcome to do the same."

Billy shook his head. "I ain't worked this hard in my whole life. I might have to go beggin' for my old job back from Sheriff Beasley."

Andy laughed. "That'll take a lot of beggin'. You didn't just burn that bridge, you chopped it into kindling and then set it on fire."

Jack grinned at the two men riding away fussing at each other. They were good men. He'd ride any trail with them. Fetter pulled him out of his thoughts.

"Marshal Sage, I don't know why you can't tell me about the other shipment."

Jack ignored him and started for the office. Fetter looked at Jack, started to follow, then looked at the mules still loaded with gold. "I'll be there shortly, Marshal," he called to Jack's back.

Pushing the door open to the small office, Jack caught Hardwick taking a sip of coffee. The marshal continued, set his cup down, swallowed, and said, "Well?"

Jack drew a fat envelope from a pocket inside his coat and tossed it on Hardwick's desk. The envelope hit, slid across the desk, and came to a stop against the coffee cup. He stepped to the potbellied stove, took the coffeepot from the top and poured himself a cup, then grabbed a chair, and moved it near the desk. He dropped into the chair, took a sip of his coffee, and stretched his long legs across the small room. "It's all there."

"Tell me about it."

"We caught the robbers. You can tell Judge Coleman they're in the El Paso marshal's jail, waiting for his decision on what to do with them. We also got all the gold back."

"From both robberies?"

Jack shook his head. "No, just the stage. Seems they're cashing in the gold for greenbacks and taking the money to the ranch. The cash from the first robbery is stashed somewhere at the ranch, known only by Elijah Rush."

Hardwick looked over the confession. "This pretty much hangs all of the Rush gang. What's your plan?"

"You wanted to put a posse together. How long would it take you?"

"Say the word, and we'll be riding out of here before dinnertime. How many men you need?"

"From what I could gather from Haggard and Victorio—"

Hardwick had been leaning back in his chair, his feet propped up on his desk. His feet dropped, and the front legs of his chair slammed to the floor. His upper body shot forward. "Victorio. You talked to Victorio? When? How'd you get away?" He looked Jack over. "You don't appear to be bleeding, and you still have your hair. What happened?"

Jack held up both hands, palms toward Hardwick. "Easy, Marshal. We ran into Victorio and about fifty of his braves while we were crossing the Mimbres," Jack continued, explaining the situation and conversation he'd had with the Apache chief.

Hardwick stared at Jack. "Boy, I've got to say, you lead a charmed life. There ain't many who could run into Victorio and still be around suckin' air."

Jack continued, "Anyway, he gave me some information on Rush's ranch. Seems it's pretty well fortified. He said the ranch house is built next to the north face of the canyon wall, but it's not built right up against it. There's some space between the wall and the house. He also mentioned a window. If a man came down the canyon wall by rope, he could make it to the window and possibly get inside."

Hardwick shook his head. "You ain't gonna find anyone who'll climb down the side of that canyon and try to slip through a window that may not be there."

Jack took another sip of his coffee and shook his head. "I'm not asking anyone to do it. I'll do it myself. Once I'm inside, I can clear the house. I'll either capture or kill whoever might be in there."

Hardwick sat staring at Jack. "And what's the posse supposed to be doing while you're climbing down that rope?"

"Hopefully not shooting me, maybe getting into the bunkhouse and barn. Whatever you do, you need to keep Rush's bunch focused on you."

Hardwick pressed both palms against the desk and rose. "Alright. Let's get this posse together."

The door burst open, and Fetter charged in. "Marshal Hardwick, what's happened with the first shipment of my gold, and when are you going to get it?"

Before the marshal could respond, Jack rose to his feet. He turned, towering over the Wells Fargo agent. "Do you have my receipt for the gold and the mules?"

Fetter slid to a stop. "I, uh . . . well, no. Davis is counting it right now."

Jack shook his head. "You left that boy with all the gold? A thief could walk into your office and steal every ounce of it. Don't you have any guards around? If it's stolen, you'll be responsible for the third loss of gold from Wells Fargo."

Fetter almost went into shock when he realized Davis was in the office with no guard. "Sorry, sorry . . ." He spun around and dashed from the office.

"And get my receipt," Jack shouted at the flustered agent.

Hardwick chuckled. "You sure have Fetter falling all over himself."

"It'll do him some good to think about his failings for a while instead of everyone else's." He turned back to the marshal. "Billy, Andy, and I need to eat, change clothes, and repack for the cold country. I'm sure it's gonna be cold up there. Also, if you could include Hank Marsden in the posse, I'd appreciate it. I need to talk to him, and I think he can take us straight to Rush's ranch."

The marshal's brow wrinkled. "He knows the ranch location? I don't know of anyone else who knows except the hands."

Jack shook his head. "How he knows isn't important, but he'll be a big help."

Jack lay warm in his bedroll, a gun gripped loosely in his hand, listening and thinking. He had to hand it to Hardwick. The marshal knew what he was doing when it came to putting together a posse. True to his word, he, Billy, and Andy had barely finished with their packing and dinner when Hardwick had ridden up to the hotel with ten deputies in tow. They were all solid men, including Hank Marsden.

Following Hank's lead, they had traveled to within a couple of miles of the Three Sixes. The attack would be set early, before daylight. If all went well, the outlaws would have no idea they were anywhere around until Hardwick opened the dance. Hopefully it would give Jack time to get down the rope to the house and window.

If he could get the drop on Elijah Rush, that might be the end of the fight. Jack rubbed his neck. This was one time he hoped they'd fight. He could feel his anger seething beneath the surface. Elijah Rush was responsible for what had happened to the schoolmarm, Mrs. Graves, and all the others who had been murdered in the robberies. Reckoning time for Rush had arrived, and Jack was bringing it.

His mind eased away from the upcoming attack to his earlier discussion with Hank. The mine owner, his partner, had made some good points and a surprising proposal. Hank had sent the gold Jack had brought from Hangman's Canyon to an assayer he used in Mesilla. The man was more of an academic than a practicing assayer, and for some unknown reason, he liked living on the Rio Bravo. He had turned farmer and was growing a vineyard, but still worked with minerals for a few friends. The gold Hank had sent the man had astonished him with its richness. After testing the ore, he found it promised to be a bonanza-class strike.

Jack heard his friend let out a honking snore. Hank had had a tough time holding in his excitement. After they had set up camp, he'd motioned Jack to walk with him into the pines. When the camp and men were barely visible between the trees, he had stepped near Jack, grasped his arm, and whispered, "With this mine, you'll never have to work again. This is the kind of strike men dream of but never see. I can't wait to see it myself." Then he'd turned so he could look Jack straight in the eyes.

"Jack, I'll buy you out right now, sight unseen. This could be a bonanza, or it could be shallow, surface only. But with my other mine doing so well, I have a lot of extra money to speculate with. I'll give you fifty thousand dollars right now, and if we strike what I think we will, another fifty thousand when I make my first two hundred thousand. I'll be honest with you, this could be the strike of a lifetime or a paltry strip of surface gold. You stand to be rich as Croesus or make only a few thousand dollars. That goes for both of us. What do you think?"

Fifty thousand, Jack had thought, *that'll buy and maintain a good-sized ranch. I've been nothing but lucky since I came out west, barring a few scrapes and bullet holes. Should I take it? If I don't and it's a bonanza, I can be a wealthy man, but what does that do for me?* He'd gazed past the pines at the men and the mountains. *This isn't bad country. In fact, I could settle down here. I know Victorio, if anyone knows Apaches, and I trust him. I could start a ranch out here. Maybe this is the place for me.*

"Jack, what do you think?"

He had snapped back to the present. "Hank, I think we have a tough day ahead of us. Let me think about it, and I'll give you my answer tomorrow."

"Fair enough," Hank had responded, and they had returned to the camp.

Jack stretched his long legs in his bedroll, adjusted his position, and pulled his hat over his face. He closed his eyes, and with the sweet smell of pines in the air, the wind providing a low rustle in the trees, Jack Sage slept.

⁓

ONE OF HIS hands had slipped outside his blankets. It felt cold, like it was lying on a chunk of ice. His eyes snapped open, and from under his hat, which had protected his neck and face, he surveyed the camp. It was still and quiet and white. The wind had settled, and his hand had good reason to be cold. It was buried under a thick coating of fresh snow. Big, soft flakes floated through the pine tops to settle on the posse. The camp looked surreal. Everything and everyone was covered with a deepening layer of snow.

He jerked his hand from beneath the snow and shook it. The flakes were dry, and except for a thin layer that had melted against his skin, they fell to the ground. He sat up, removed his hat and shook it, tossing snow in all directions. A clump of it found its way into Billy's face. He jerked up, spluttering, and stared at the surroundings just as Jack had done, then he poked Andy. With their movement the camp came to life.

The moon, hidden behind a wall of snow and clouds, gave little help. Darkness and silence filled the mountains. It would be a cold start this morning. No fire and no coffee. As soon as everyone was up and saddled, they'd be on their way. Jack had a longer distance to travel than Hardwick and the rest of the posse. He moved to Pepper, brushed the snow from the horse's head, neck, and back, and saddled the animal.

Hank hurried to him. "Let me come with you, Jack. I can give Hardwick directions. He won't have a problem, but you need to get to the rim area, and you have a long way to go. If you make a wrong turn, it could mess up this whole operation."

In the snow and darkness, Jack could barely make out his mining partner. "Sounds like a good idea to me if you can give them good directions, but we need to get moving now."

Hank took off at a jog, disappearing into the ever-moving wall of snow.

Andy appeared like a wraith through the white curtain. "Jack, you want us to come with you? There's no tellin' what or who you might run into."

"Thanks, Andy, but since he knows the way so well, I'm taking Hank. Any more people, we stand the risk of being discovered. You and Billy stick with Hardwick and keep those Rush gang members pinned down. Stay safe."

Andy gazed at Jack a moment longer. "Luck." He turned and headed back into the snow.

Hank reappeared on horseback. "I've given directions to Hardwick. You ready?"

Jack swung up onto Pepper. The big horse bowed his back, but thought better of it and settled down. Riding out, Jack pulled up next to Hardwick. "Marshal, good luck to you. Hopefully when we see each other later today, we'll be celebrating."

Hardwick nodded. "My hope, too. Good luck to you. This snow's not gonna make that rope any easier to crawl down."

Jack touched his hat and followed Hank into the timber.

The riding was slow and quiet. The steps of the big horse were silent in the dry snow stacked on top of the pine needles. Hank guided his horse unerringly through the timbered country, and Jack followed close enough to easily make out the outline of man and horse. At one point the falling snow lightened, allowing Jack to see past the horse ahead.

They were on a trail. The edge dropped almost straight down for five hundred feet. It appeared they were at the head of a canyon. From here the walls sloped steeply downward. In the distance, he could see the ranch house at the mouth, and the canyon wall rising above it. Though the height of the wall decreased drastically from where Jack currently rode, it looked to be at least a hundred feet from the rim to the house. The clouds closed in, and the snow returned. Jack urged Pepper forward. He had no desire to lose Hank in the soft white falling snow.

Sensing the difficulty, Hank pulled to a stop and waited. Once Jack drew closer, he heard Hank cluck, and the horse continued forward. They rode for another thirty minutes, and Hank stopped. He turned to Jack. "Right after it cleared, we made it across the canyon head. Now we're no more than a few hundred yards from where you need to anchor your rope."

"Good." He motioned forward, and Hank continued. Snow or no snow, today would see the end of Elijah Rush's dreams of living off other people's wealth. Jack knew little about the man's previous life before coming to Silver City, but he didn't really care. Rush was a thief and a killer, and a leopard rarely changed its spots.

Hank pulled up again. "This is it, Jack." He pointed to his left. "Any of these pines will do to anchor your rope. It's almost straight down, so the slope won't help you at all."

Jack swung off Pepper and eased in the direction Hank indicated. Sure enough, the edge came into view. Stepping to the brink of the drop, he looked over. There was no house. All he could see was snow falling straight down. There was no visible bottom, just falling snow passing his head and continuing until it vanished in the whiteness. He moved back.

"You're sure the house is directly below us?"

Hank gave an emphatic nod. "Dead certain. See the big rock at the edge, just past the massive pine? That's the place I watched Rush and his bunch from. You can swing your rope around the pine, and when you get to the bottom, you'll be a few short steps from the window."

Before untying the ropes from his saddle, Jack looked across Pepper's back at his friend. "Hank, I think I'll stick with you on the partnership. I appreciate what you wanted to do, but we're in it together."

Hank started to speak, but Jack stopped him with an uplifted hand. "If anything happens to me, you take half of my portion and include the rest with the five percent I've already given the Pratts."

Hank grinned at Jack. "Alright, partner. We'll either make a little or be rolling in gold. Luck to you."

"And you." Jack began untying the rope from his saddle. It was time. He had brought many vicious men to justice, but Rush was probably the worst. The thought of his dead wife and son, and their murderer, drifted across his mind. *With the exception of one.*

21

Jack anchored the rope around the pine tree, tied the others together, and slowly began letting the end over the cliff. He was beginning to grow concerned he might not have enough rope when it went slack. Just enough. He let the rest of it out and checked both his Smith and Wessons, ensuring they were fully loaded. Jack gave a single wave to Hank and went over the edge.

He curled one boot around the rope, stepped on his instep with the other to form a friction brake, and began lowering himself. He hadn't traveled past the length of his first section of rope when a shot rang out below. It was followed by a barrage of fire blasting through the snow. He couldn't tell whether it was coming from the house, barn, bunkhouse, or the surrounding posse, but *he* was committed and continued his descent.

The rope was wet. He had coated the palms of his gloves with sticky pine sap before beginning his descent. It clung to anything it touched, giving him a better grip on the rope, and should work well throughout the length of his hazardous, downward travel.

The snow continued to fall around him, but his confidence grew. The sticky sap was working exactly as he'd hoped, and he was making good time down the rope. At this rate, he'd soon be on the ground.

His right hand slipped.

The jerk and twist of his body yanked the rope from between his boots.

He plummeted toward the unseen ground below.

The grip of his left hand and the pine sap were the only things between him and death.

He fell, spinning, the rope whipping and banging him off the cliff wall. With one of the rebounds, he managed to grab the whistling hemp with his right hand. With every ounce of strength he could muster in his forearms, he clenched the rope between his two big hands. His palms burned like hot coals were being pushed into them.

He slowed.

Swinging his leg around the whipping rope, he at last maneuvered it between his feet and jammed the sole of one boot into the instep of the other.

He stopped, hanging in a white tunnel of snow.

Jack's heart was beating like an Apache war drum. He hung, slowly rotating in space, no sky above or earth below. He took a deep breath.

More shots rang out, snapping him back to his senses, and he began to work his way down the rope. Glancing down, he thought he could make out an outline. It was the roof. Then the roof became clear, and he could see the barn and bunkhouse. *The snow's letting up,* he thought.

A shot rang out, and chips from the cliff face struck him in the shoulder. He had been spotted. He loosened his grip again, carefully this time, maintaining control of the rope, and his body shot downward. Another shot struck the cliff. It hit right where he had been, but he was safe, below the roofline of the house. Jack slowed his descent and watched the ground rise.

He touched and felt the ground beneath his feet. Holding the rope to steady himself, he allowed his shaking legs to relax. The moment of truth was at hand. He had been looking forward to this meeting, and now it was here.

Just like Hank said, the window was only a few short steps from where his feet touched the ground. He flexed his hands. They still burned like fire. If they were going to stiffen, it would be a while. He had time. He drew one of his .44s and started forward.

There was a fierce gun battle toward the front of the house. He could hear shots, yells, and cries of pain. Ricochets whined across the yard and down the canyon. Bullets thudded into solid timbers. Men were fighting and dying out there. The sooner he reached Rush, the sooner the battle would be over.

Jack pulled his hat off and peeked around the edge of the window. The first thing he saw was a file cabinet, then a plush chair behind a big wooden desk, a couch, and a couple of wing-backs. Looking down, along the edge of the window, he made out a wooden cabinet. He watched for a few seconds, holstered his six-gun, and moved to the window, grasping the bottom.

With the application of his first pressure, nothing happened. He wondered if the window had ever been opened and why in the world anyone would put one here against a rock face. It wasn't his concern. He was just glad they had. Jack levered all of the strength in his legs and shoulders, driving upward. The window didn't stand a chance. It released reluctantly, squeaking fiercely as it rose high enough for him to shove himself inside.

Jack dove headfirst over the cabinet, into the room. He drew his weapon even as he was still in flight. Upside down, he could see a stunned gunslinger step into the doorway and level his six-gun. Jack fired from an inverted position, struck on his left shoulder, and rolled, earing the hammer back again.

The .44-caliber slug caught the man under his chin and knocked him back into the hallway. As he fell back, he dropped the revolver and grabbed his bloody throat with both hands. Jack gave the man only a glance, knowing the outlaw was more concerned with stopping his life's blood from pumping out of his body than shooting anyone else.

Jack stepped past the man. The hallway gave him a choice. Most of the gunfire came from his left, and where there was gunfire, there were shooters. He took four steps to his left and stopped. He could see into the large room with four windows. They looked over a wide porch and toward a shabbily built barn. Four men, one at each window, were firing into and across the yard.

Jack had never made a habit of shooting a man in the back. He stepped into the room. His booming voice sounded over the gunfire. "Drop your guns, boys."

The men spun at his words. It was obvious by their actions none intended to follow his orders. The closest fella was a tall drink of water. He swung his Winchester, attempting to bring it to bear on Jack. He was fast, but getting that long gun around was a difficult task, and he wasn't going to make it. Jack fired, hitting the man in the shoulder. He staggered and fell back through the window onto the porch. His body jerked from the strike of multiple slugs, and he collapsed.

Another of the gunmen had made the mistake of jumping erect in front of his window, and a bullet from the treeline caught him, knocking him to the floor.

The man at the far window was quick. He whipped around, bringing his Colt into alignment, and fired first. Jack felt the pull of the bullet under his left arm as he pulled the trigger, striking the man in the chest. He could see the gunman was clinging to his six-gun and trying to bring it up again, but he still had to worry about the one remaining shooter in the room. He recognized him as another Rush.

He had deep-set eyes and heavy eyebrows, features Jack had learned to recognize as belonging to a Rush, but he wasn't the old man. This must be another of his boys. The shooter's Colt flared, and Jack felt the bullet slam into his right leg, turning him, but he was able to keep his feet. He fired before the man could get off another shot.

His bullet caught Rush high in the left shoulder, turning him away from Jack momentarily, but he immediately began turning back. Jack fired again, striking the man in the right shoulder. The gunman's fingers flew open like they were on springs, and the gun dropped to the floor, but Jack wasn't out of the woods yet.

The man at the far window, with the chest wound, was still trying to bring his weapon up.

"Leave it be," Jack said. "I don't want to kill you."

The gunman said nothing, but kept raising his revolver. Jack took aim and fired, striking the man in the forehead.

Jack drew his remaining .44. He wasn't as good with his left hand, but he was good enough in quarters as close as this. He moved sideways to ensure he was clear of the hallway and windows. "Hardwick? You out there?"

A call came from the yard. "Yeah. You alright?"

"I'm fine. I don't know if there are any more in here, but I've got four down inside and one lying on the porch."

"Those shooters were the last of the holdouts. We caught the fellers in the bunkhouse red-handed. They never fired a shot. We're coming in."

"Make it cautious like. I haven't seen old man Rush or the older fella. They could be where they can shoot. I'll wait until you get in before I start looking around."

Running boots sounded on the porch, and the front door burst open. Billy charged in with Andy right behind him. They checked the men. All were dead except Boone Rush, who had a bullet in each shoulder and lay on the floor, cursing them and Jack.

Hardwick came in behind Andy. He motioned for several of the other men to clear the remainder of the house. Turning to Jack, he said, "You're hit."

Jack sat in a brown leather wingback chair, which had much of the stuffing blown out of it. "Yeah, would you believe it?" He pointed to the dead man who shot him. "He shot me in my bad leg. This is the second time I've been hit in that leg."

Hardwick pulled up a chair and called to Billy, "Would you head for the kitchen and see if you can round up a touch of coffee for an old man? That'd really hit the spot."

Billy looked at Jack. "You want some, too?"

Jack grinned at him. "If you're going to the trouble for one, you might as well make it two."

Dr. Pratt strode into the room. "Let me take a look at that leg." He turned to several of the men. "Would you fellas please grab a few more logs and throw them in the fireplace? Also hang blankets over the broken windows so we can warm it up in here."

"Sure, Doc," they replied in unison.

"Now, let's take a look at that leg. Take off your coat."

Jack stood and removed his heavy coat. When he did, the doc pointed at his left side, just beneath his armpit, where blood was soaking his shirt and vest. "Looks like someone got you there."

Jack looked down at the blood and shook his head. "I hate inside gunfights. Men get jammed up tight in a small place, and everyone's liable to get shot."

Billy returned with the coffee. Jack took a long sip. The hot bitter liquid felt good going down. "Thanks, Billy." He turned to Hardwick. "Did you get the old man?"

The marshal shook his head. "Haven't seen hide nor hair of him. I don't know how he managed to do it, but he's nowhere to be found."

Doc Pratt examined Jack's ribs first. "Just a scratch. I'll slap on some ointment and a bandage, and you'll be good as new. Now let me look at that leg."

"Don't tear my long johns, Doc. I've got a feeling I'm gonna need them before this is over."

"Then get your trousers down so I can get a good look at that leg."

Jack pulled down his trousers and his long johns, exposing an ugly gash where the bullet had dug a channel along the outside of his right leg. The doctor examined the bleeding wound while looking over the old wound. He cleaned and bandaged the leg in short order. "Looks like that leg's taken a bit of punishment."

Jack nodded, not feeling like explaining to anyone. He stood, pulled the long johns and trousers up, and looked around the room. "We have anyone else shot up?"

Doc Pratt had been watching him when he pulled up his trousers. "What's wrong with your hands?"

Jack could feel them stiffening. He worked his fingers a bit, shook his head, and said, "Nothing."

The doctor frowned. "Don't give me that. Get back over here, sit down, and take off your gloves."

Jack started to argue, and thought better of it. *It'll take less time,* he thought, *if I let the doc do his work than if I argue with him.* He sat and began pulling his gloves off. It felt as if they were sticking as he pulled each from his hand. He knew what that meant.

Both palms were raw and bloody. It was a good thing he had worn his gloves. Without them, the flesh would've been pulled from his palms. The doctor said nothing, but began cleaning his hands. Once they were clean, he bandaged them, looked at his work, and sat back. "You have any more holes I don't know about?"

"That's about it, Doc."

Hardwick leaned over and stared at Jack's hands. "Those hands'll be slowing your gun-handling down for a while." He rose. "Like I was about to say before Doc got so excited about your hands, we've got a couple of Rush's gang winged and a couple of our boys." Hardwick looked around the room they were in. "'Ceptin these fellers you took care of and the feller on the porch, ain't none of theirs dead, and none of ours was killed. Good thing too. If those men in the bunkhouse had decided to fight, there'd be a lot more dead around."

The doctor had moved on to Boone Rush, who was stretched out on the floor. Jack walked over and stared down at the outlaw. Rush looked up at him and began cursing. Jack listened for only a second, then pulled his .44, leaned forward and shoved the muzzle hard against the outlaw's forehead. "I'm going to tell you once to close your filthy mouth. You only open it to answer my questions. Do you understand me? Nod your head if you do."

Boone Rush, eyes wide like saucers, nodded his head, trying to get away from the pressure of the muzzle against his forehead.

"Good." Jack calmly slid his revolver back into its holster, leaving a well-defined ring on Rush's forehead. "Where's your pa?"

Rush shook his head.

"Speak up."

"I don't know." He turned his head toward the doc. "I could use a drink or laudanum, something to kill the pain."

"Where's his room?"

Rush looked out the window, ignoring Jack's question.

"Boone, don't make me draw again. You won't like it if I do."

"Alright, alright, his room is the big one in the back."

Jack stared at the wounded Rush lying on the floor in a pool of his own blood.

Rush watched Jack watching him. Finally he couldn't stand it. "I'm tellin' the truth. Please get me a drink."

Jack glanced at Doc Pratt and nodded. "If you think it's alright." He turned and headed to the back. *Something's not right here. We should've had him. No one could have gotten to him ahead of us.*

Striding from the room, his slight limp more prominent than it had been, Jack headed for Elijah Rush's bedroom. Billy and Andy followed. Once there, he saw a disheveled room with several of the posse making it worse. An armoire stood next to a dresser against the far wall.

Jack looked out the window. The snow had completely stopped, and the clouds were breaking, showing fragments of a deep blue sky. The wind had picked up from the north. He expected it to be clear and cold tonight. He glanced to the right and caught a glimpse of a building adjacent to the bedroom, joining the back of the house.

He turned from the window, looked around the room, and walked to the foot of the large bed. "Flip the mattress," he told Andy and Billy. Each went to a side. They raised it vertical and allowed it to fall, coming to rest against the wall. Nothing was under the bed.

Jack turned and opened the armoire behind him. There were only a few pieces of worn clothing hanging. A run-over pair of old boots sat in one corner, but nothing else. It was hard to tell anyone lived here. Certainly Rush used this bedroom only for sleeping. He stepped back and closed the door.

The wind was getting higher. You could hear it outside, and he could feel it on his legs. He turned to leave the room and stopped. *Why can I feel the wind on my legs inside this bedroom?* He leaned down and held his hand at the bottom of the armoire. It was set on short one-inch legs, but he could feel a draft flowing under it. He looked closely at the floor and could see an arc of barely visible scratches. Marks where the end opposite the dresser had been pulled from the wall. He grasped the end and pulled.

The armoire moved easily, gliding away from the wall and exposing a hole about three feet in diameter. He pulled it farther and stepped behind it. "Look at this, boys."

Billy, Andy, and the other two men had stopped their searching and crowded around the armoire, staring at the gaping hole. Jack looked through the hole to the storage shed on the other side. He could see through the interior wall to another cabinet, which had been pushed out of the way. "Get Hardwick." Jack drew his Smith and Wesson and stepped through the two walls.

Looking around, it was easy to see how the men had escaped. They had waited until everyone headed for the house, moved the furniture, slipped through, and pulled it, by a handle screwed onto the back, into its original position. Rush had thought of everything.

In the dust of the storeroom floor, he could see their tracks lead through the room to a back door. It opened, just enough for a man to squeeze through, against the face of the cliff. *That's why they have a space between the house and the cliff,* Jack thought, *to allow the door to open and give them an escape route.* A feed bin sat next to the door with its lid up. *They simply stashed their money in the feed bin. Rush wasn't concerned about any of his gang taking the money because they all knew he'd kill whoever stole from him.*

Hardwick had followed Jack through the hole. "Not the slickest escape route in the world."

Jack nodded and pointed toward the two sets of tracks in the snow from the door and disappearing into the pines. "Of course, at the end of those footprints, we'll find a corral and barn where they kept horses, and I'll remind you, Marshal, it was slick enough to fool us."

Hardwick nodded. "You've got me there. You headin' after 'em?"

"I am. I hired on to stop Elijah Rush, and I aim to do it."

Billy and Andy had joined Hardwick and Jack. Andy spoke up. "We're going with you." Billy was nodding in agreement.

Jack turned to the two men and shook his head. "Not this time. This is a one-man job. You both know I'll travel faster if I travel alone. I thank you for your willingness to pitch in. Andy, you've got a business to run. I imagine folks are getting tired of not having you around, and if you're gone too long, another gunsmith may move in on your territory."

Andy grinned. "I'm not much concerned about that, but I

imagine folks are ready for me to open again." He extended his hand. "I'm obliged for the break in monotony, Jack. I can tell my grandkids about riding this trail."

Jack gingerly took the deputy's hand, careful of his. When he released it, he turned to Billy. "I don't know what you have in mind, and I can't speak for Marshal Hardwick."

Hardwick spoke up. "I can. If you want a job, you've got one. Stay as long as you like. I have a feeling when the next election comes along, the sheriff might have some strong competition."

Billy chuckled. "Thanks, Marshal. I think I'll take you up on the job. I'm not one for sitting around." He turned to Jack. "It's been an experience. Thanks."

Jack nodded. "Both of you are good men. I appreciate what you've done. Andy, you can leave your badge with the marshal when you get this bunch back to town. Good luck to both of you.

"Now I've got to be riding. Hank should be showing up soon with my horse. Then I'm heading after Rush. The two of them can't get far."

22

J ack had found the lean-to barn where Elijah Rush and
Micah Durant had hidden their horses. It was located
behind a thicket of aspen. A man could pass it on the
opposite side of the thicket and never know it was there.
They had chosen their hiding spot well.

The tracks of the two horses led south, for the border. *You're
never going to make it, Rush,* Jack thought. He guided Pepper after
the tracks, staying well to the east side and in constant timber. He
didn't think either of the two men would ambush him. Rush was
too set on escaping. He'd left his boys to deal with the law, and
had run out on them. *With a father like that,* Jack thought, *those
boys never had a chance. Now the living ones will hang along with
their father, if I don't kill him first.*

He continued on the trail, dropping out of the tall timber. The
shorter piñon and cedar took over, and as the elevation continued
to decrease, the landscape turned to bunch grass, mesquite, and
greasewood.

A jackrabbit leaped out of the trail, causing Pepper to shy to
the left. At the same time a .44 ricocheted off his saddle horn, and
Jack dove, hitting the rocky ground hard. He knocked his Stetson

from his head when he slammed into a good-sized rock, causing a deep gash. Like any head wound, it immediately began bleeding profusely, running into his left eye.

He lay still. *Maybe I can fool them,* he thought. *Turnabout's fair.* He hadn't expected an ambush. He didn't think Rush had it in him. He figured the killer would run like the scared jackrabbit that had caused Pepper to shy. *Thank goodness that rabbit scared Pepper. If the horse hadn't jumped, the bullet would have hit me low in the belly. I'd be a goner.* The question now was whether he could fake out the ambushers.

Jack lay for what seemed at least an hour. He knew his muscles were stiffening. He hoped he'd be able to move fast enough when the time came, or all this would be a waste.

Time continued to click by. Jack's coat covered his hand, but unfortunately, when he hit, like an amateur, he had allowed his weapon to be knocked loose. But it was his good luck to have the tail of his long overcoat fall over his hand. He felt a jagged rock and, with almost imperceptible movement, gripped his only available weapon. He continued to lie motionless. He couldn't get to his other revolver because it was under him. He'd have to move to get it, and then the drygulcher would know he was faking it. The warmth of the sun increased as it rose.

At last, he heard rocks rattle. Jack lay motionless, listening to the scrape and crunch of his ambusher moving closer. He willed his body to wait. Moving too soon would spell his death.

Jack could hear the man's breathing and felt the coolness of a shadow over his face. He heard a knee crinkle the bunch grass next to his side just before a hand gripped his shoulder.

The man shoved to roll him over, and Jack used the leverage to swing. He was going for the man's head, but the instant his eyes opened, he saw the muzzle of a rifle inches from his forehead. He redirected the rock to the forearm of the Winchester, smashing his assailant's fingers between the forearm and the rock.

The blow on the rifle's forearm moved the barrel inches to the side. The man pulled the trigger, blasting the .44 slug into the rocks six inches from Jack's already damaged head. He felt the rock fragments explode into the top of his head, and his ears were screaming in pain, but those minor discomforts mattered little. He was alive and had the older man and his rifle in the grip of his massive hands. He ripped the rifle from the man's hands.

Even in the moment of success, he saw doom rising in the speed of his ambusher. The older man was fast. When he saw Jack had control of the rifle, he released it, stepped back, and went for his handgun. He was smooth. The man's left hand was bleeding, but he was paying it no mind. His right hand flashed, in a smooth arc, from the rifle to the butt of his Colt.

In the meantime, Jack was levering a round into the Winchester and reversing the barrel toward the man. He was in an awkward position, still half-lying on the ground, using his right leg and core muscles to hold his body high enough to work the Winchester's action. He saw the Colt slip from the old holster. It slid easily out and began tilting toward him the instant the barrel cleared the edge of the holster.

Jack almost had the Winchester's muzzle turned. Only another moment. As soon as the muzzle covered a portion of his target, he pulled the trigger. There was no squeeze, it was a solid pull, straight back. The Winchester roared again. Somewhere in a remote part of his mind, he was thankful that he could hear the blast of the rifle. At least the shooter hadn't deafened him permanently.

He saw the bloom of blood on the man's left chest. It hit the ambusher just before his muzzle found Jack. The impact drove the shooter's body to the left, throwing his shot off, and Jack could feel the disturbed air as the chunk of hot lead flew past his head, level with his eyes. There was no time to think or rejoice over the miss. His right hand slapped the lever, throwing the empty case out and driving a live round into the chamber. This time, he had the advantage. "Drop it," Jack said.

Jack could swear the man smiled as he brought the Colt around, trying to get it on target while he eared the hammer back. An instant before the Colt's muzzle came to bear, Jack fired again.

This time he wasn't rushed. He was on one knee and had the Winchester's muzzle centered on the man's chest. The trigger pull was more like a squeeze, and the bullet traveled no more than ten feet, striking the gunman in the center of his chest. He stumbled back and sat down on the rocks.

Jack levered another round into the rifle, continuing to cover the man, and moved toward him. His opponent watched him through bright green eyes. Jack reached down and took the gun from his hand and then kneeled next to the man. "You're Micah Durant."

Durant nodded and coughed. He reached up and grasped Jack's bandanna, pulling it off and staring at the puffy scar. "They shouldn't have done that to you. I told Elijah to leave you alone. I told him you were bad news, but he wouldn't listen." He coughed, blood on his lips. Using Jack's bandanna, he wiped his mouth, looked at the result, and gave Jack a slight grin. "Guess you'll need a new one. I've got some money in my vest pocket. Take it, and buy yourself a fine silk one. I won't be needing it."

"Where's Rush?"

Durant gave his head a weak shake. "He's gone. His horse went lame, and he took mine."

"And you're out here protecting him?"

Durant shook his head again. "Crazy, isn't it." A hard bout of coughing hit him. "It's a long story. Bottom line is I owe him. Long time ago."

"Where's he headed?"

"Somewhere he hopes he'll be safe and rich. Even as . . . a boy, he was always scared." Durant was gasping for breath.

"How long have you been with him?"

"Seems like my whole . . . life." Durant smiled again and released a long sighing breath.

Jack watched the bright green eyes turn dull and fade. He sat staring at the older man. "Micah Durant, I don't know why you stayed with him, but you don't strike me as a fool. You're going to have to pay for what you've done, but standing by a friend oughta count for something."

He stretched the man out. There was no time to bury him. He had to catch Rush before he harmed anyone else. He emptied the man's pockets, finding a few dollars in coins, like he had said, and a chew of tobacco. He put them both in his vest pocket and took the man's Colt, gun belt, and rifle.

Jack laid the beat-up hat across the old face and walked over to Pepper. Wrapping the belt around the holster, Jack shoved it into his saddlebags and slid the Winchester into his bedroll. He pulled two cookies from the bag, refastened it, and gave one to Pepper while he munched on the other. Once they both were finished, he poured his hat half-full of water and let his horse drink. When Pepper was through, Jack swung into the saddle, tipped his hat to Durant, and bumped Pepper into a lope. Rush's tracks were a clear, straight line across the Chihuahuan desert. His head hurt, not like pain from a wound, but more like a throbbing headache.

Less than two hours had passed when Jack made out the single rider ahead. As he drew closer, he could see the horse was unsteady, the big man kicking at him, but still on his back, with a large suitcase. Jack shook his head and, once within range, pulled Pepper to a halt, stepped down from his horse, and looped the reins around his forearm. He raised his rifle and put a round far enough in front of the horse so as not to spook him.

Rush started kicking the animal, and Jack put another round in the same place. The outlaw leader turned in the saddle, stared over his shoulder at Jack, and pulled his horse to a stop. He sat clinging to the suitcase.

Jack placed his foot in the stirrup and began to put weight on his left leg when another excruciating headache caused him to wince and lean on the saddle. He clung to the saddle horn and leaned against the cool leather. Gradually the headache dissipated, leaving his strong body weak, and his legs shaking. *What is this?* he thought. *I've never had headaches. Why now?*

After a few moments he felt his strength returning. He continued into the saddle and rode, his rifle resting comfortably across his legs. Reaching Rush, Jack eased to one side so the rifle's muzzle covered the outlaw, and pulled Pepper to a stop. "Did you really think you'd get away with all that money?"

The big man glared at Jack, watching him and his Winchester's position. "Listen, Sage. You're a reasonable man. There's enough money here for the two of us. I'll split it with you fifty-fifty. Just let me go. You can tell them you couldn't find me. Tell them anything." Rush looked back up the trail as if he expected other riders to show themselves.

"Get off the horse."

"What?"

"I said get off the horse. Can't you see you're killing that animal." Jack raised the rifle.

Rush climbed down and set the suitcase on the ground beside him.

Jack noted the small leather strap that secured Rush's .44-caliber Remington in its holster was released.

Jack could feel something wet on the side of his head. He touched it and looked at his hand. Blood. The rock and the shards from the rifle blast had done a number on his head. He was probably bleeding from several of the rock strikes.

Rush noticed the blood. "I guess Micah is dead."

"He is. He got too close."

Rush shook his head. "He was a good man. We've been together for a long time."

"That's how you repay him?"

Almost belligerent, Rush said, "What do you mean?"

"It's not safe being kin or a friend of yours. You leave everyone to fend for themselves while you skedaddle away like a nervous little kitten."

"You can't talk to me like that. Micah wanted to stay, and so did my boys. I've taken care of all of them, and they appreciated it. This was their way of paying me back."

Jack couldn't believe what he was hearing. He thought, *Rush, you must be crazy as a loon. You seem to believe your own lies.*

"So it was alright for you to ride off and leave your friend to ambush me all by himself? By the way, if you had done it together, you probably would have gotten me."

Rush, his eyes drawn so tight one wondered how he could see out of them, continued to glare at Jack. "I've told you, he wanted to stay."

"Give your horse some water."

"What?"

"Rush, I'm getting mighty tired of having to repeat everything I say to you. Give your horse water."

"In what?"

"You're not that stupid."

"If you didn't have that rifle trained on me, you wouldn't be talking to me like that."

Jack said nothing. He reached down, checked to make sure his six-guns were loose in their holsters, and slid his rifle back in its scabbard. He thought he caught a quick grin on Rush's face, but it was gone as quickly as it appeared.

"You're a prideful man, Jack Sage."

"And you're going to hang, Elijah Rush."

The two men were thirty feet apart, Rush on the ground, holding his suitcase, and Jack sitting relaxed in his saddle.

"I told you to give your horse water. Pour it in your hat."

"I don't think so. Your horse looks big enough to carry me. I think I'll take him."

Jack grinned at the man's audacity and then winced. The headache was coming on again. *Not now,* he thought. He had always known he would someday face a faster man who was just as accurate. But Rush wouldn't have to be faster if Jack's headache overpowered him. He concentrated on forcing the headache away, and miraculously, it began to fade.

"I'm going to kill you, Jack Sage, and then ride out of here on your horse."

Jack was positioned where he could easily see his back trail, and he saw a cavalry troop top a distant rise, coming directly for them. "If you're going to ride out of here on my horse, Rush, you'd better get to it. A troop of soldiers just topped the last hill I came over."

"What?"

Rush jerked his head toward the nearing soldiers, and before he turned back, his gun hand was moving. He was fast.

Jack marveled at the speed of the big man. He, even though he was also big, was always surprised when he saw a big man do anything quickly. But his surprise didn't affect his speed. His only thought was the safety of Pepper.

Even as he drew, he rammed his spurs into Pepper's flanks. Jack never used spurs on his horses. He would bump his horses to get them moving, or cluck, but that was it. So the big chestnut, surprised at the pain, leaped forward. Jack had the reins in his left hand and yanked the horse to a stop, throwing his left leg over the saddle and kicking his right foot out of the stirrup. He dropped down on the off-side of Pepper, facing Rush. Pepper's movement had taken them to an angle that cleared the outlaw's trembling horse.

Rush was faster than Jack, but his bullet sailed through the space Jack had been, across the Chihuahuan desert, to bury itself harmlessly in an innocent greasewood. His eyes grew wide as he saw flame and smoke pour from Jack's Smith and Wesson.

"Nooo!" he screamed.

Jack's bullet plowed into Rush's chest, knocking the man backward. He stayed on his feet and held his Remington. Jack watched him look down at his chest in disbelief and start up with the gun again. Jack was ready. He fired and began walking toward Rush. Drawing closer, he fired again, again, and again. Rush absorbed the lead, finally dropping to his knees. With both hands, he tried to bring the Remington in line with his opponent. Jack drew his remaining Smith and Wesson and emptied it into Rush. He was taking no more chances with this killer.

The troop rode up to Jack. He was standing over Rush, his six-gun trained on the man while he methodically eared back the hammer and snapped the weapon on an empty chamber again and again.

The lieutenant held up his hand to halt the troop, and said nothing. He remained motionless in the saddle. Finally he spoke. "Major Sage? Major Sage."

Jack, through the pain from his head, heard his name on the second call. He looked up at the lieutenant, then at the bullet-riddled body of Elijah Rush. His mind slowly broadened to the outside world. He dropped his smoking weapon into its holster.

He felt no pity for Rush. The man had caused the death of so many innocent people. He had treated his friend and his children like chattel. A picture of his dead wife and little baby filled Jack's mind, and he thought, *If my child had lived, I would have treated him like a treasure.* The thought floated away, and he looked up at Lieutenant Burns. "He drew on me."

"We saw it all, Major. He definitely drew first."

Someone in the ranks whispered, "He won't do that again."

The lieutenant turned to the sergeant riding next to him. "Sergeant, dismount the troops and take care of that trooper."

The sergeant snapped a salute. "Yes, sir. Dismount."

The cavalrymen stepped from their horses, their gear rattling.

Jack walked over to the horse Rush had been riding. The heaving of the animal's sides was decreasing. He rubbed the big head, which drooped in exhaustion. "Lieutenant, do you think you could get one of your men to water this fella? He's had a hard time."

"Yes, sir, Major Sage, I certainly can." He looked at the sergeant, and the man ordered a private to water the horse.

"Walk with me, Lieutenant." Jack turned toward Pepper. Halfway there he stopped, as if his mind was catching up with him. He drew and unlatched each of his six-guns, snapping the barrels down to flip out the empties, and dropped six fresh cartridges into the chambers of each weapon. After loading, he dropped them into their holsters and continued to Pepper. He examined the wounds where his spurs had dug into his horse's sides. "Sorry, boy. I know it hurt, but maybe it kept you from getting that slug in your belly."

"Major, we have some good salve for that. If you'd allow me, I'll have one of my men take care of your horse."

Jack nodded. "I'd be obliged, Lieutenant." He pulled his canteen from the saddle and took a long drink. The water seemed to help the throbbing pain in his head. He removed his hat and poured a portion of the water over his head. He could feel his scalp burn when the water hit the cuts.

The lieutenant stared at Jack. "Major—"

"Stop with the major, Lieutenant. I'm a civilian. Call me Jack."

"Thank you, Jack. Your head's in bad shape. I have a trooper along who's very good with wounds. Would you mind if he takes a look?"

Jack's headache was worsening. "Lieutenant, I wouldn't mind at all, but I think I'd better sit down before I fall down." Jack started down, and his legs gave way. Burns grabbed his arm, preventing him from slamming into the ground again. Jack watched the bright afternoon sun dim until it looked more like twilight. He smiled. He liked this desert. It was pretty country. Maybe he'd settle down. Maybe he'd start a ranch with the money from the gold mine. Maybe . . .

23

J ack awoke in the Fort Bayard infirmary. The first thing he noticed was the headache was gone.

Fort Bayard, manned by the U.S. Cavalry, was located ten miles east of Silver City and provided what little protection they could to the miners, against the marauding Apaches.

A nurse sat at his bedside. When his eyes opened, she rose, went to the end of the room and knocked on a door. It opened. A man dressed in a white coat hurried toward him.

"Major Sage, I am Dr. Winston. How do you feel?"

Jack threw back the sheet, glad to see he was at least dressed in a nightshirt, and looked around for his clothes. He put a hand to his head and found it covered with bandages down to his eyebrows. "What happened? The last thing I remember was the shoot-out with Rush, and Lieutenant Burns."

"You lost consciousness. You weren't hit by any bullets, at least any that hadn't already been taken care of, but there were several rock shards embedded in your skull. I would be interested to hear how it happened, but that's not important right now. One of the shards of rock penetrated your skull and applied pressure to your brain." Winston raised his index finger in front of Jack's eyes and began to move it back and forth. "Watch my finger. This is one of several tests we need to do before we can give you a clean bill of health."

Jack stared at the man. "You were saying a rock stuck in my brain? Did you get it out?"

"It didn't stick in your brain. It penetrated your skull and applied pressure but did not penetrate the protective covering of the brain, and yes, we got it out, and you are sewn up. It will take a while for the bone to knit back in place. Just make sure you don't get hit in the head while that is happening." Martin chuckled at his own dark humor.

"Could the rocks have caused a really intense headache?"

The doctor nodded. "The one penetrating through your scalp and into your brain definitely could have. It could have also caused unusual behavior. Are you experiencing any such thing now?"

Jack shook his head, threw his legs over the side of the bed, and began to sit up.

Seeing Jack attempting to rise, Dr. Winston placed his hand on Jack's shoulder to apply enough pressure to push him back into bed. "Now don't get excited."

Jack locked his stare on the doctor. "Doc, I appreciate what you've done for me, but I'm finished here. Get my clothes. I'm leaving, and if you'd like to use your arm in future surgeries, you'd better remove it from my shoulder."

The doctor glanced at Jack's face to see if he was joking. When he saw the deadly serious gray eyes staring back at him, he jerked his hand away and straightened. "Well, Major Sage—"

"Get this straight, Doc, I appreciate your help, but I'm not hanging around here another minute. Have someone get my clothes, or I'll find them myself, and stop calling me major. I'm no longer in the army."

Hearing Jack's threatening tone, an orderly stepped to the doctor's side in case he needed help. The doctor turned to him. "Get Mr. Sage's clothes and gear, please."

At that moment the door exiting to the veranda opened, and a colonel, accompanied by a civilian, entered the infirmary. Dr. Winston straightened. The colonel was a well-proportioned man with wide shoulders his dress uniform did little to hide. His hair had smatterings of gray under his campaign hat. The faded saber scar across his forehead was dim but did alter the direction of his wrinkles. "And how is your patient, Captain Winston?"

"Colonel Newell, good morning, sir. He seems to be recovering well and is . . . uh . . . quite lively. He demands his clothing and desires to depart our service."

The colonel approached Jack's bedside, eyeing Jack with hard blue eyes. "Major Sage, you do understand you are on an army base?"

Jack held the gaze. "That's hard to miss, and I'm no major, so I'm not under your command, Colonel."

The orderly stood behind the colonel and the doctor with Jack's clothes in his hands, including his six-guns.

"Furthermore, I'm leaving." Jack swung his long legs over the side of the cot and stood. His movement forced the colonel to step back, allowing the big man, wearing only a nightshirt, room to stand. "Colonel, are you going to throw me in irons, or allow me to leave?"

The colonel took another step back and to the side, providing an opening for the orderly. The younger man stepped forward, handing Jack his clothing and guns.

"Much obliged, Private." Since no one was moving to allow him privacy, he stepped into his long johns, pulled them up to his waist, and buttoned them. Next, he slipped the nightshirt over his head, exposing his muscular chest and the wounds he had on his upper body. He dropped the nightshirt on the bed and shoved his arms into his long johns. Once he had them in place, he shrugged a couple of times to get them positioned and then buttoned the remaining buttons. He continued dressing, pulling on his trousers next.

"*Mister* Sage," the colonel said, "when you are dressed, would you be so kind as to join me and my associate in my office? I want to emphasize, this is not a command, but a request from one gentleman to another."

Jack slipped his shirt over his head and began tucking it into the waist of his trousers. "Thank you, Colonel, I'd be pleased to."

The colonel and the other man turned and left the infirmary. Jack sat on the edge of the bed to pull on his boots. He wouldn't let anyone know, but he was feeling a little light-headed. Hopefully, it would go away. "Doc?"

The doctor had been watching the colonel leave the room. "Yes, Mr. Sage?"

"You think you could get someone to bring me a glass of water? I'm danged near as dry as that desert out there."

The orderly spun around at Jack's request and hurried off.

"Of course. I am sorry I didn't think of it when you awoke. It will be here right away."

Jack slipped his other boot on and stood. The room tilted slightly and stabilized. The doctor had been watching his eyes. He stepped forward, a hand reaching out. "Are you alright, Mr. Sage?"

Jack waved the hand away. "Yeah, Doc. I just need a drink."

When the tray showed up, Jack didn't finish drinking until the orderly had filled his glass three additional times. He set it on the tray and nodded to the orderly. "Obliged. That hit the spot."

Finally, Jack picked up his gun belt and swung it around his waist. Once fastened, he adjusted the holsters slightly to ensure they were in the right position, and slid the Bowie knife's scabbard close to his right six-gun. "I think that's it." He extended his hand to the doctor. "Much obliged, Doc. I don't mean to be abrupt, but I'm not one for hospitals, never have been. I appreciate your help."

The doctor took his hand. "I'm always glad to do it, Mr. Sage. Be careful for a while. You could experience bouts of dizziness and headaches. Be prepared for them. They should go away in less than a week."

"How do I find the colonel's office?"

"When you go out the door, it'll be the first building to the left."

Jack picked up his bloodstained Stetson. The blood was all over the inside of the hat and had soaked through the felt to the outside. *Dang it,* he thought, *there goes another hat. I don't think I've seen anyone as hard on hats as me.* He stepped to the door and looked back. "Thanks again, Doc." He pulled the door closed and smelled the fresh air. There were no antiseptic smells, only the smell of greasewood, honeysuckle, and a hint of horse manure. At the end of the tall porch, the honeysuckle drooped around the building's corner.

It was in the direction of the colonel's office, so he stopped at the vines and pulled one of the small yellow trumpet-like flowers from the vine. He turned the tiny end to his mouth and sucked. The faint sweet honeysuckle taste he remembered so well as a boy glided over his tongue. He pulled another and repeated the action, then turned away, his lips drawn into a smile, and strode toward the steps leading up to the tall porch of the office.

Jack climbed the steps and entered. Several desks filled the room. They formed an aisle and also a barricade that allowed the sergeant major, sitting at the nearest desk to the colonel's office, control of the entry.

When Jack entered, the men working at the desks looked up, and the sergeant major stood. "Good morning, sir. You must be Major Sage."

Jack walked down the short aisle to the desk. "I am, Sergeant Major. Colonel Newell asked me to stop by."

"Yes, sir. He's waiting." The man turned, knocked twice on the door, opened it, and announced Jack.

"Send him in."

The sergeant major stepped back, allowing Jack access to the room. He walked in to see the colonel and the faintly familiar stranger waiting. Both were standing.

"You may close the door, Sergeant Major, and I'll be taking no visitors."

When the door had closed, the stranger gave Jack a quizzical look. "You don't remember me, do you, Jack?"

Jack searched his memory. There was something there, but he couldn't pull it out. "I feel I know you, but for the life of me, I cannot place your face. I do believe it had something to do with the war."

"Good. Yes, it did."

The colonel picked up his hat. "Mr. Sage, I have officers I need to address. I will be gone for a while." He glanced at the stranger. "You have my office as long as you need it." He strode to the door, opened it, and was gone, pulling it closed behind him.

"Let's sit over here," the stranger said, indicating a long couch. On the table in front of the couch was a pot of steaming coffee, along with cream and sugar. Also a plate was stacked high with sugar cookies.

"Would you care for a cup of coffee, Jack?"

"At this point, I'd probably kill for one."

The man, smiling, jerked his hands in front of him, palms forward. "Far be it from me to get in your way. Please help yourself. The colonel told me his wife made these cookies. He said she would be mightily disappointed if any were returned to her."

Jack poured two cups of coffee and loaded his with cream and sugar. The stranger picked up his cup, nodded thanks, and sat at the opposite end of the couch. Jack placed two large cookies on an empty saucer and set his cup and saucer at the edge of the table near him, dropping onto the couch. He brought the cup to his lips and let the sweet, hot liquid course down his throat. The concoction hit the spot. He had no idea how long he had been unconscious, but knew it had been several days, and he was hungry. With half a cookie in his mouth, he turned to the stranger, chewed, swallowed, and said, "So how do we know each other?"

The stranger let a conspiratorial grin edge across his face. "Do you remember the raid you led for General Grant, hitting the railroad junction?"

Jack's eyes lit up. "You're the spy who was waiting at the railroad. You set all of the explosives, but I never knew your name."

The man laughed. "It wouldn't have meant anything. It was an alias. My real name is Carter Schofield." He pulled an envelope from his inside coat pocket and handed it across the sofa.

Jack took the envelope and examined it. Turning it over, he stared at the seal on the back, the President of the United States. "What is this, Carter?"

"I can tell you, and then you can read the letter inside, or you can read it while you're drinking your coffee."

Jack removed his Barlow knife from a pocket. "You tell me, and I'll get this opened while you're talking."

Carter took another sip. "Jack, you made a great impression on President Grant. You impressed him first with your performance in the war, and he has kept an eye on you since. He knows you have been instrumental in several coups in South America and cleaned up a few towns from Mexico to Texas. He also knows about your rescue of those kidnapped young girls in Texas. He believes you are not only the man for the job, but the *only* man for the job."

"Just tell me, Carter. I'm no politician. I don't need buttering up. What does he want?"

He slipped the blade of the Barlow into the edge of the envelope, making sure it was clear of the letter, and drew the sharp edge across the paper.

Carter watched Jack open the message. "He, the president, wants you to work for him directly. You will be operating as a United States Marshal, but you will answer only to him, through me. I will relay his orders for as long as you are willing to work for him or as long as he is in office. When you decide it is no longer worth the risk, you can call it quits, and there will be nothing but gratitude from the president."

Jack slid the letter from inside the envelope. It had been folded in thirds. He opened it to see the signature he remembered so clearly of Ulysses S. Grant. He scanned the letter, amazed at its content.

When he was finished, he raised his stunned gaze to Carter Schofield. "You're to be my liaison with the president?"

"Yes, and I am honored he offered me the opportunity to again work with you. I am authorized to provide you with anything you want or need. I will deliver his messages and will smooth the way politically, where possible. I will remain in the background. You can on occasion call on me to assist if you need additional muscle." He made an obvious scan of Jack. "Although I doubt that will ever be necessary. However, an extra gun might sometimes come in handy."

Carter Schofield stopped speaking. "What do you think so far?"

Jack swallowed the portion of cookie he had been chewing. "I'm ready. Whatever he needs. We need law in this country. The sooner we get it, the sooner men like me will no longer be needed."

"Good. We're going to be working together for what I hope will be a long time, so I'm going to be honest with you, Jack. Until this last report from Lieutenant Burns, I was totally on board with the president." Schofield paused and stared out the window at the swaying cottonwood tree outside the colonel's office.

He turned back to Jack. "From his report, it sounds like you were totally out of it in this last gunfight with Elijah Rush. The president needs a man thinking, aware of his surroundings. Can you explain what happened? The lieutenant said you emptied two guns into Rush and were standing there snapping an empty weapon at a dead man. He had to call you twice to get your attention."

Jack gave a pensive nod. "I didn't know how many times he called to me, but I vaguely remember all the rest. The doc was telling me they had to dig a shaft of rock from my brain. I received that little present from Micah Durant, Rush's employee. He had been left to ambush me, unsuccessfully, but his miss was close enough to send this piece of rock into my brain. Just before the gunfight with Rush, I was having powerful headaches, which I've never had before. Dr. Winston said it was caused by the rock, and I should recover completely."

Schofield nodded in thought. "The brain is a funny thing. Now I understand." He reached for the plate of cookies and took one. He silently chewed on the cookie and studied Jack.

Jack said nothing.

"Good," Schofield said, "that's behind us. So tell me, are you on board with this operation?"

"Yep. When do I start?"

"Right now." Schofield drew another envelope from his coat and handed it to Jack. "This will explain who and why."

Schofield sat silent while Jack opened the letter and began to read.

When he was finished, he looked up. "I liked General Franklin and Warren. I'm sorry to hear they were murdered."

"Yes. The general was a good friend of the president. The local sheriff, in Wyoming, is claiming it was done by Blackfeet."

"Sounds like the president doesn't believe him."

Schofield shook his head. "Not a word. In the president's last meeting with General Franklin, the general was excited about how the Blackfeet were accepting him and his family. He had helped them, and they were grateful." Schofield pointed at the letter. "You understand, finding the killers is only part of your assignment."

"I do, and I have to admit, it's hard to believe the general's wife intends to continue ranching with her three daughters and daughter-in-law. She seems to be biting off way more than five women can handle."

Schofield nodded. "I agree, but Mrs. Franklin is one head-strong woman. The general tried to get her to stay in the capital at least until spring, but she wouldn't do it. She says she and her girls are going to run that ranch and make a go of it."

"I wish them luck." Jack shook his head. "But they've got a long row to hoe and a tough one."

"That's where you come in. You're to give them whatever aid they require."

Jack laughed. "And find the killers."

"And bring the killers to justice."

Jack finished his fourth cookie. "Wyoming's a long, cold way north, especially this time of year."

"It is. I, along with Lieutenant Burns and his troop, will be accompanying you as far as Santa Fe, then it'll be up to you. I'll fill in a few more details along the way." Schofield paused. "Oh, I forgot. There's one more thing." He reached into the pocket he had taken the letters from and took out a small case. He tossed it to Jack.

It was an attractive black, round, leather case, hinged at the top. He looked it over and opened it. Lying on a purple satin bed was a shiny new badge, much like the one he wore, but on the outer circular band, United States Marshal was engraved. It was bright, no scratches. *I'll take care of that,* he thought. Jack lifted the badge from its case, removed the beat-up and tarnished badge from his vest, and slipped the new one in place.

Jack Sage, with his bloody hat in his hand, his head, ribs, and right thigh covered with bandages, stood. "We're burning daylight, Carter. Let's hit the trail."

Hit the trail with Jack Sage as he rides into his next adventure.
Book 5:
FIVE WOMEN AND THE STAR

AUTHOR'S NOTE

I hope you've enjoyed reading *The Hanging Star,* the fourth book in the Jack Sage Western Series.

If you have any comments, what you like or what you don't, please let me know. You can email me at: Don@DonaldLRobertson.com, or fill in the contact form on my website.

www.DonaldLRobertson.com

I'm looking forward to hearing from you.

BOOKS
A Jack Sage Western Series
STRANGER WITH A STAR
WITHOUT THE STAR
RETURN OF THE STAR
THE HANGING STAR
FIVE WOMEN AND THE STAR

Logan Mountain Man Series
(Prequel to Logan Family Series)
SOUL OF A MOUNTAIN MAN
TRIALS OF A MOUNTAIN MAN
METTLE OF A MOUNTAIN MAN

Logan Family Series
LOGAN'S WORD
THE SAVAGE VALLEY
CALLUM'S MISSION
FORGOTTEN SEASON
TROUBLED SEASON
TORTURED SEASON

Clay Barlow - Texas Ranger Justice Series
FORTY-FOUR CALIBER JUSTICE
LAW AND JUSTICE
LONESOME JUSTICE

NOVELLAS AND SHORT STORIES
RUSTLERS IN THE SAGE
BECAUSE OF A DOG
THE OLD RANGER

Printed in Great Britain
by Amazon

54852502R00137